Advance praise for
My Enemy . . . My Brother

The drama of Hanna Shahin's life is living proof that the grace of God is surprising in its reach and truly liberating in all of its results. Rarely have I read the testimony of someone so uniquely chosen by Christ for the sake of the gospel.

Stephen Davey, M.Div., STM, D.D.
Senior Pastor, Colonial Baptist Church
President, Shepherds Theological Seminary
Principal Bible Teacher, Wisdom for the Heart

When God in His sovereignty wants to do something great he starts preparing the right man from an early age. Such was the case with Moses, David, Moody and many others. Hanna is another one of God's workmanship for such a time as this. With the turn of every page you will be thrilled, amused, brought to tears and laughter as you witness God's hand in the life of a boy, a man, a husband, a father, a skilled gospel broadcaster and above all, a great man of God who loves Jesus and would give his life for Him.

Henri Aoun
Director of Affairs
LifeAgape International

My Enemy . . . My Brother is the amazing story of a Palestinian boy born and raised in Jerusalem. The world would consider those who are neighbors to this boy to be his enemies but for the author of this remarkable life story, by the grace of God, those potential enemies have become his brothers. This testimony was an eye opener for me to better understand the challenges Palestinians face in that part of the world.

Jürg Löliger, M.S., Ph.D.
Corseaux, Switzerland

What an amazing turn of events to see the life of my younger brother unfold before my very eyes, from tears of sadness and heartbreak where I still see him crying as we would leave him at the orphanage to tears of joy and pride at how God has molded his life.

Salem Shahin, M.D.

There is not a day that goes by without some news from the Middle East. Many peoples are now tuning it out. They say, "We will never understand all of these problems in Israel and Palestine." In this book, *My Enemy . . . My Brother,* Hanna Shahin has made that part of the world come alive. You will not be able to put this book down.

Dr. Michael Youssef
The Church of the Apostles

Peace is a term repeated frequently in Scripture. Can there ever be peace between a Palestinian and a Jew? Hanna's life and ministry certainly gives hope. His story is a fascinating read of how God took a young boy and molded him into a choice and productive servant who preaches and models peace through His grace.

Tom Lowell, D. Litt.
Chairman, Trans World Radio board of directors

It is a privilege and an honor to endorse the book of my dear friend and brother in Christ, Hanna Shahin. As you read this book, I pray that you will also be inspired and motivated to pray and be generous in helping our brothers in the Middle East for the glory of our Great Father, our Great Savior, and High Priest, Jesus Christ, to whom is the honor, the glory, and the praise forever and ever, Amen.

Tuomah Sahawneh, M.D.
Oneonta, Alabama

MY ENEMY...
MY BROTHER

GOD'S GRACE
IN THE LIFE
OF A PALESTINIAN

HANNA SHAHIN

PUBLICATIONS

Fort Washington, PA 19034

Dedication

To my 117-year-old father, who gave me the space to be myself; my four sons, who stretched my horizons; my brothers, who believed in me; and above all to my wife, Evelyn, the love of my life, who stood with me through thick and thin. All by the grace of God!

My Enemy . . . My Brother
ISBN: 978-0-87508-998-0

Copyright 2009 Hanna Shahin

This printing 2009

Published by CLC Publications

U.S.A.
P.O. Box 1449, Fort Washington, PA 19034

GREAT BRITAIN
51 The Dean, Alresford, Hants. SO24 9BJ

AUSTRALIA
P.O. Box 2299, Strathpine, QLD 4500

NEW ZEALAND
10 MacArthur Street, Feilding

Unless otherwise noted, all Scripture quotations are from *The New King James Version* of the the Bible, copyright © 1982 by Thomas Nelson, Inc.

Printed in the United States of America

Contents

Foreword

By Joel C. Rosenberg

The book you hold in your hands is, at its core, a love story—one of the most beautiful and powerful I have ever read.

It is the story of God's extraordinary love for a Palestinian boy in Jerusalem, a boy who grew up lonely and sad and afraid until one day Jesus Christ personally reached out and took this little boy into His arms and told him, "I have loved you with an everlasting love; therefore, I have drawn you with lovingkindness" (Jer. 31:3).

It is the story of a young man who becomes transformed by Christ's love, a young man both called and compelled to share the good news of that powerful love and amazing grace with his fellow Palestinians, and eventually with the entire Arabic-speaking world.

It is a story I suspect will touch your heart as it has touched mine, and my hope is that it will move you not only to pray faithfully for Hanna and his family and his team, but also for the Palestinian people and the entire Muslim world, that all might know Jesus Christ in a real and personal way.

I first met Hanna Shahin nearly two decades ago at a church missions conference in the Washington, D.C. area. He and his Egyptian-born wife, Evelyn, had come to talk about how powerfully Christ was moving among Muslims, drawing them into a personal relationship with Him in numbers never before seen in human history. The Shahins explained how God was using radio broadcasting to beam the gospel over the heads of the Arab governments who opposed the message and into the hearts of Arab men, women and children so hungry and thirsty to know that Christ really loved them and had a wonderful plan and purpose for their lives.

My wife, Lynn, and I were transfixed. We were newly married and new to Washington. We had long been fascinated with the history and future of the Middle East. But mostly what we knew was Jewish and Israeli history, given my Jewish roots. Honestly, we had never thought much about God's specific love for Arabs. Neither of us had grown up to hate Arabs in general or Muslims in particular. But we hadn't personally known any Palestinian or Egyptian followers of Christ. We hadn't really studied the Scriptures carefully enough to see God's love for Israel's neighbors, and her enemies. But I believe the Lord brought the Shahins into our lives, in part, to help open our eyes.

We bonded quickly at that conference, and our friendship has grown and sweetened over the years. We have prayed for Hanna and Evelyn. We have invested in their ministry. We have wept with them when hardships have come. And we have rejoiced when the Lord has done great and mighty things in and through their lives—which is often!

For years, I encouraged Hanna to carve out time from his schedule to write his story. I can't tell you how thrilled I am now that he has. Indeed, I thought after all these years that I knew his story. But the truth is I have learned more about Hanna, more about Evelyn, and more about God's love and mercy through this book than I could have imagined. I have been blessed. I know you will be too.

When I think of Hanna, I often think of the words of Jesus in Matthew 23:37: "O Jerusalem, Jerusalem, you who kill the prophets and stone those sent to you, how often I have longed to gather your children together, as a hen gathers her chicks under her wings, but you were not willing." From time immemorial, God has loved the people of Jerusalem. Tragically, the people of Jerusalem have not always loved Him.

This is the story of one son of Jerusalem who was willing to accept Christ's love and be gathered to His heart. May his tribe increase.

Joel C. Rosenberg
Washington, D.C.
June 1, 2009

Joel C. Rosenberg is founder of The Joshua Fund, a non-profit organization dedicated to blessing Israel and her neighbors in the name of Jesus. He is also the *New York Times* best-selling author of five novels and two non-fiction books, *Epicenter* and *Inside the Revolution: How the Followers of Jihad, Jefferson and Jesus Are Battling to Dominate the Middle East and Transform the World.*

1

My *Via Dolorosa*

I NEVER was very interested in celebrating my birthday. Perhaps part of the reason was that I didn't discover my true birth date until I was in my late teens. My attitude did not stop Evelyn, my wife, from forcing a celebration on me when she could. One very special birthday stands out. Here again it was the ingenuity of my wife that made this birthday celebration memorable. She invited the team we worked with and threw a surprise party for me when I turned forty.

Fourteen years later I would acknowledge and celebrate my birthday for the last time. It was a personal decision, the result of a major crisis in my ministry. Before getting to that phase of my life, though, let me recall the early years.

I was born to Shehadeh and Wadia Shahin, a Palestinian Christian couple whose roots are vague, and whose history is shrouded with secrecy and speculation. Of the many contradictory accounts of my family's background, a particularly telling version places the origins of my parents' families in South Lebanon, which they fled because of religious persecution.

The story has it that one of the ancestors of either my

father or my mother was the only girl in her family, and very beautiful. I do not know much about this girl, only that she probably lived four or five generations before I was born. A Muslim young man had wanted to marry her, but in keeping with their strong religious and cultural traditions, her family refused. Christians were only to marry Christians.

The young man's family was influential, however, and insisted that this Christian girl marry their son or face the consequences—at best, harassment, if not persecution; at worst, death. Faced with these options, my ancestors had no choice but to move away, finding refuge in the small Christian village of Rafeedia in the north of Palestine. It is also thought they may have been the first settlers and given the town its name. This is where my family comes from: a tiny town in Palestine, which has never made the news and probably never will.

At the time of my birth, people in the Middle East lacked basic necessities. Growing up, I don't remember seeing such luxuries as a toothbrush or shampoo. This is not to say that we did not clean our teeth or take a bath. Instead, we faced the material scarcity in our daily lives with resources we had in abundance: simplicity and imagination. To clean our teeth, we used salt; we used homemade olive-oil soap to wash our hands, bodies and just about everything else.

But we lacked many other things as well—electric lights, heaters, even shoes—and our imagination could only take us so far. I suppose the limitations were in themselves something of a virtue; after all, since we did not know these things existed, how could we really miss them? Admittedly, they were not all basic needs.

One such nonbasic item that comes to mind is a camera.

With my poor memory, photos would have done miracles in helping tell my story. They would have provided a backup, a trigger point enriching my faded background with colors, images and emotions. I realize too that they would have brought back memories of pain and want more readily than those of happiness and plenty, but pain and happiness are inextricably part of my story. Regretfully, without any photos, I have to conjure up images of my past as well as my memory allows, and rediscover the emotions that correlate with them.

My father, at age 117, is the oldest living man in present-day Israel/Palestine. Perhaps he never saw the need for a camera because his memory is so vivid (or so he claims). During the brief years I lived with him as a teenager, he would talk to me in detail about his parents, revealing many painful stories from his youth that refused to die, picking at the memories as one picks at a scab that refuses to heal.

He kept on repeating, almost with anger, but surely with dismay, how his father made him leave school at a very young age, and not because the family needed money. My grandfather made his son work at the Samaritan convent, doing all types of odd jobs. This is where my father mastered the Greek language.

My grandfather made all the decisions—he even picked out my father's wife for him. My father was married against his will to a woman he had never laid eyes on until she stood at the wedding altar. Feelings and emotions became mere irrelevances; my father was an only son, and his first duty was to have more sons. The survival of the family name trumped all other concerns.

My father seldom spoke to me of his first wife, my mother.

She remained, through his silence, a ghostly figure, distant and cold. It was probably because he did not enjoy speaking about her. He partly pitied her, at least now that she was long deceased. He had harsh words for both his and her parents, as neither family liked the other much, or possessed the wisdom and grace to help my father and mother improve their relationship. Their troubled married life had been far from ideal, yet they had seven children, of whom I was the youngest. I have often wondered why they would bother having seven children—or any children at all, for that matter.

About the time I was born—my father cannot remember whether it was immediately before or soon after—my mother fell sick with throat cancer. For a while, they tried to treat it with a medicinal herb. (Herbal remedies are not new to Palestine, and they are dispensed for just about anything, from headache to cancer; they may alleviate headaches, but are useless against cancer.)

None of the traditional treatments worked, and as my mother began losing weight and getting sicker, my father called on the help of local doctors—as much as his meager income permitted. More time was wasted as weeks turned into months, and months into years. My bedridden mother's hope for recovery grew dimmer, until one day my father heard about a hospital in Jordan where she could perhaps be treated. He took her there, but by then it was too late, and very little could be done for her. I was five years old, or so I am told, when my mother died.

Yet, for all that my father said about his parents, his childhood, or his marriage, he could provide no visual record of it. I have never needed proof, of course, but I have always longed to see a photo, to know these people who were a part of me but nothing more than strangers. I especially wished for a picture of my mother, but to my utter disappointment, there wasn't a single one—not even a wedding photo. It was as if she never existed. I was thankful to have a father at least, though even he only started to become real for me when I was twelve.

I don't remember knowing much when I was five years old. I knew my name was *Hanna*, which is Arabic for John. I knew I had at least three brothers, Salem, Joseph and Abe. Abe was the oldest and I only saw him occasionally. Every once in a while, he would come home wearing a black robe, stay a few days, then leave. I had no clue where he was coming from or where he was going. My two other brothers, Salem and Joseph, were mostly home at the time. We all lived in one spacious room on the first floor of an old building whose hallways were permanently damp and dark.

My brothers and I didn't have any money to buy toys, so we would invent games to keep ourselves occupied. The going logic was that if it did not cost money, it could be a pastime, whatever "it" happened to be. A basic version of "it" saw Joseph and Salem compete at dipping their heads into a large bowl of water and counting to see who kept his head submerged longer. A more technically accomplished version of "it" involved bringing home two circular staves sliced off an empty metallic barrel then tying the two pieces together in the hope of keeping them standing on their edge. And *voilà*! They had reinvented the bicycle.

Salem was three years older than I. I can still see him walking me to the old building where I went to school, in the middle of what seemed like a sea of sand. It was the Christian Missionary School. I did not understand what the

name meant, nor did I care. Salem held me by the hand all
the way there. School was where I was supposed to be, according to him—definitely not according to me. When all I
wanted was to stay with him, all he wanted was to rid himself of me, to drop me off and go.

I still see myself crying after him with my nose running,
and using my shirt sleeves to wipe my nose. It was the same
scenario every morning: He would force me into the class; I
would run out after him, but he would shove me back in
again, this time with a stern look on his face. I would stand
by the window crying, my nose still running. It is amazing
how long a nose runs in situations like these. I was homesick
and lonely. I was missing something, *someone*. I craved a family, but my family had more urgent things to think of.

I wondered why I was taken to school; I didn't learn a
thing. Only later did I realize that I was not sent to school to
learn, but simply to have a place to go, because there was no
one at home that could care for me. The school was the
closest thing to a day-care center, except it was lifeless and
loveless. I don't remember how long I went to the Christian
Missionary School, but it was certainly long enough to leave
these imprints on my memory.

But that was only the beginning. My *Via Dolorosa* was in
the making, and the Christian Missionary School was only
my first station. The next station was in Bethany, on the
Mount of Olives just outside Jerusalem, in an orphanage. At
the age of five or six, I had no say and could not choose what
happened to me. I simply had to follow and obey. I have no
recollection of who took me to the orphanage, or how I found
myself there, but for the next six or seven years I lived with
women robed in black. The large white hats they wore on

their heads looked like butterflies. Only their faces were visible, as their ears and necks were covered. Years later I learned they were Sisters of Charity, and they lived up to their name—or at least Sister Agnes did.

Sister Agnes (the only sister in the orphanage whose name I remember) was more like a real sister to me than anyone I had ever known. She did not mind my sitting next to her when she played the piano, and she often gave me an extra piece of bread between meals. It is hard to imagine what such little things can mean in a child's life. I cannot recall how many other boys were in the convent orphanage at the time, but I do remember how little, if any, individual attention was given to any one child. To be allowed, and even at times invited, to sit next to Sister Agnes was a rare treat. Her angelic smile was so comforting.

I have just one photo from my years at the convent—a black-and-white image of myself as a smallish, plump boy of about six or seven, wearing shorts and sandals. I am flanked on each side by two of my older brothers: Solomon (whom I came to know years later) and Salem. That picture comforts me, for it is tangible proof that I had family—a caring family. And yet, that same picture also haunts me: Where was everyone else? Why was I exiled to that place?

So many contradictory emotions swell in me whenever I look at this painful memento of my past. There, captured in black and white, is all the loneliness of my childhood, staring me in the face. And yet I treasure this picture, even though part of me wants to tear it into a million pieces. Of course, what I really want to destroy are the circumstances, the reasons and logic that placed me there, at the orphanage. The same questions and doubts surface again and again. Why did I not only have to live without a mother but also without a father or a family? Over the years, I have been given various reasons and explanations, but none are fully satisfying.

My years at the convent were marked by waves of isolation, need and resignation. Solitude was my daily bread. While there were other boys on the compound, each lived on his own little island. We ate together, but never truly shared a meal; we slept in the same room, but each in his own lonely bed. There were no outings, no sports except running around in the dusty outdoors. Because of my years there, I still avoid crowds and shy away from attention. I wonder what happened to the other boys who were my companions in solitude during those years. I wonder if their lives, like mine, were also scarred.

My years at the convent included physical as well as emotional deprivation. The Mount of Olives can be extremely cold during the winter months. I hated getting out of bed in the morning. I dreaded the cold water with which we had to wash our hands and faces. And then there was the daily walk to school in downtown Jerusalem, three miles each way. It was so cold my skin would crack and bleed; I still remember the open sores on my hands and knees. In those days, I did not know gloves existed.

Rain or snow, wind or dust, I only ever wore sandals on my feet. My classmates at the day school all had shoes. I didn't know why I didn't, and I wanted a pair, but I had no idea where to get them. Everyone else at the convent had sandals, probably the sisters also. It wasn't until I was fourteen that I had my first pair of shoes. As a result, material things don't really matter to me. I am content with one pair of shoes, even at my age.

I remember an old, stooped priest who would visit once in a while. He always carried a big black cloth bag in his right hand—actually, he didn't carry it, but pulled it behind him as he walked. When he came, we had a feast, for his bag was filled with thinly sliced bread. Although it was stale and beginning to harden, I had good teeth, so I did not mind eating the bread. I could always dig my teeth into it and chew.

He also brought us a tasty yellow cheese. It too was hard, and dry around the edges, which had faded to brown, but the heart of every slice retained a yellowish softness that was truly delicious, and unlike anything we were fed at the convent. That cheese was in the autumn of its life, and remembering it now fills me with melancholy. I still miss that cheese the priest used to bring. On days when my nostalgia overpowers me, I leave slices of Swiss cheese out in the sun, in an attempt to rediscover my past. It's never quite like that old cheese I loved, but it serves as an anchor to my past, and makes me grateful for what I have, and had.

As I think of the foods we were given each day at the orphanage, one staple of our meager menu stands out: powdered milk and water. For many years, I thought milk only came in powdered form. That was the only milk I knew, and I detested it. Every morning a full glass of powdered milk would be waiting for us ominously at the breakfast table. It was a daily battle to find someone willing to drink my glass, and conducting negotiations undetected by the watchful eyes of the sister attending required much skill and determination. At times I resorted to giving away what little money I had just to get rid of that milk. Despite the high price, I considered it a great bargain.

Another lasting memory I have of my time with the Sisters of Charity is the celebration of Christmas, which began on Christmas Eve. The boys of the orphanage were led into a large room adjacent to the kitchen which we were normally not allowed to enter. This was the "bathing room"— not quite a Turkish bath, but its next of kin. We took turns undressing, and the women who worked in the kitchen, with some of their older daughters, took turns bathing us with hot water and soap. We were being readied for Christmas Day.

The next morning we were given "new" clothes—actually, second-hand clothes collected from donors in Europe, or possibly from second-hand stores in Jerusalem. But they were new to us, and that was good enough. We were then taken to church. One of the sisters stood at the door of the church, checking to make sure that our sandals were dusted off, our shirts tucked in and our hair combed. There were important people attending Mass with us on Christmas Day, and we had to look clean and presentable in front of them. It was the sisters' chance to show us off to these men.

We knew from their colored robes and from the way we were made to address them that they were no ordinary men. We kissed the back of their hands, and the sisters themselves treated them with the utmost respect. These men were important and honored church officials, who sat on assigned elevated seats at the front of the auditorium.

Mass itself was nothing out of the ordinary, even on Christmas Day. After hearing the story year after year of Baby Jesus, the journey of Mary and Joseph from Nazareth to Bethlehem, the star, the shepherds and the wise men, it had all become commonplace. It was the presence of those church officials that made it special.

Not quite special enough for me, however. None of that—the hot bath, the special Mass, the men in their robes, the new clothes—was what I waited for with bated breath every Christmas. What I was really after was the cup of hot chocolate and the single sugar-coated bun we were given for Christmas. Year after year I pleaded for a second cup and a second bun. Year after year I was denied. Even on Christmas Day, it was a life of deprivation and poverty.

Why couldn't we have hot chocolate and sweet buns for breakfast every day? I wondered. I wished I had the money to buy them. But there were no miracles, and I couldn't escape my sentence: I would have to wait another three hundred and sixty four days before I could hope to have another cup of hot chocolate and another sugar-coated bun.

The grinding reality of deprivation and isolation soon lead me to what was perhaps an all-too-natural reaction: resignation. I could do nothing to change my situation, just as I had done nothing to find myself in the orphanage in the first place. I hadn't chosen to go to Bethany, and I hadn't chosen to stay there. There are many things one doesn't choose in life.

So I daydreamed to escape the reality around me, and I hoped, and even prayed, for my life to change. Yet dreams, hopes and even prayers can only take a child so far, and it was with cruel regularity that the sisters' morning bell woke us up and brought us back to our dismal reality. We were still in Bethany, day after day, year after year, with no end in sight, so I learned to accept my destiny.

I was one of the smallest and youngest boys in the compound. As if that wasn't enough, I was also one of the poorest, making me an ideal target for other boys to bully. I figured that my best chance of survival was to keep to myself and avoid conflict at all cost, even when I was in the right. I didn't quite succeed every time. I can still see myself flying off a staircase and landing several feet below after a bully threw his school bag at my legs. Other boys, as well as one of the sisters, came to my rescue, helping me to my feet and taking me to the infirmary. I was bruised and bleeding from various cuts on my arms and legs, but thankfully I hadn't broken any bones, though it certainly felt like I had.

To this day I avoid conflict. I like to think it is because I am a peacemaker, but when I am truly honest about my motives, I recognize that what really motivates me is fear of conflict and tension. If I don't go after my brother when he wrongs me, it's not because I'm living the Beatitudes, but because I'm not willing to confront and risk losing him. Being left alone, in peace—or at least in the absence of conflict— is more important to me than being right. It is not because I have such a generous spirit, it's simply because my young world, my inner world, did not include violence.

Religiosity was another defining aspect of my years at the orphanage. Prayer and the liturgy were the markers of time. Reciting Hail Mary or the Lord's Prayer as I worked my way through the rosary at least once a day was a mere fact of life. I coveted acceptance, both on this side of heaven and on the other.

I attended Mass every day at my school in downtown Jerusalem, and on Sundays, a local parish priest came to the orphanage to lead Mass at our church in Bethany. By the time I was twelve years old, I was regularly serving as an altar boy. My desire for acceptance, far more than a desire to be or do good, is what compelled me to become an altar boy. I wanted to impress others. The way I saw it, there was nothing to lose and everything to gain from this simple service, and, if nothing else, I was sure that God would take pity on an altar boy and forgive him for passing his dreaded glass of milk to someone else at the breakfast table.

In the course of my duties, I memorized the Latin Mass by heart. To this day my wife occasionally catches me distractedly reciting the *Pater Noster Qui Es In Caelis*, "Our Father who art in heaven."

Being an altar boy proved to be more stimulating to my senses than I had anticipated. My position granted me access into the sacristy with the priest, after Mass. That was the privilege that truly set me apart. Mass itself did little to stimulate me, and neither did Catholic doctrine, much of which I did not understand. Transubstantiation is but one example: I did not particularly care to understand how bread turned into flesh or wine into blood. The only wine I cared about was in the inner chambers, with the priest, and my ambition only went as far as some day having a small sip of it.

The rich smell of incense that filled the air at Mass also transported me to another world, far away from my reality at the convent. I miss the smell of the incense, and the feelings it evoked in me. But above everything else associated with the Mass, I enjoyed the Gregorian chants. They sounded heavenly and pure. For those few minutes when I was allowed to sit and listen, the singing seemed to melt my pain away. I was more ready to accept my lot and be thankful. I was in solitude, but not lonely.

My natural aversion to violence and conflict, my religiosity, and above all my need to be accepted and loved, led me to see myself, by every human measure, as a good boy. I was *un bon enfant!*

Thankfully, I was a good student. In fact, for many years I was the *best* student in my class, finishing every year with top grades. Year after year, the French Catholic school I attended inside the walled city of Jerusalem honored me with a *Prix d'Excellence*, a medallion pinned on my small chest by the principal of the school, a Jesuit monk. I could wear it every day from the end of one school year to the beginning of the next. That small medal was a source of great pride for me, and probably still is today. Perhaps because of those early years, achievement and success became highly prized goals in my life. When I was eleven, a prize even more wonderful than the medal awaited me at the end of the school year: Because I had achieved the highest grades again, I was allowed to skip a grade. I guess both my age and my grades helped move me ahead, since until that year, I had been the oldest one in my class. Those days were over, and I prided myself on that too.

In the summer of 1959, when I was twelve years old, I got to spend one or two weeks at my father's house, or, rather, in my father's *room.* My father and my brothers Joseph, now seventeen, and Salem, just three years older than I, all lived together in that one small room. One of my two sisters, Marie, was also visiting, and had come from her Catholic girls' boarding school. Marie was four years older than I, and she had been sent to her school in the same way I had been shipped out to Bethany, and probably about the same time too.

The space where my father and my brothers lived was a

stand-alone room among others in a half-public courtyard. A small kitchen was to one side of it, while the bathroom was located around the corner from the kitchen. It was not quite public, but not private either. There were a couple of neighbors that lived to the right and left and shared that same bathroom, as well as the courtyard.

To me, my father's room felt like a palace! The lack of space did not matter, quite the contrary: I coveted less space, not more. I needed closeness, not distance. My own sons always wanted their own rooms, and frequently rebelled against the confines of shared space. I, on the other hand, wanted to sleep with my two brothers in the one and only bed. My father worked at the Knights Palace Hotel in East Jerusalem, and slept there, so it was just us kids at home. Those two weeks I spent cramped in my father's room in Jerusalem that summer were the best weeks of my young life.

Alas, they came to an end far too quickly, and my euphoria turned to distress as the day of my return to the orphanage approached. I cried uncontrollably. I pleaded with my brothers to keep me, but my pleas went unheard. More reasons. More excuses. More wrongs to correct wrongs. As much as I may have been a victim, they also were victims of their circumstances. They probably didn't know how to do any better, and I didn't understand the full extent of their powerlessness, their limitations, whether financial or practical. I could see the pain in their eyes. I knew they loved me, and I loved them, but that only made it harder to leave.

Finally, I gave in and dragged myself out. My brother Salem held me by the hand, but not as a mother would hold the hand of her son to comfort him. I was held because he knew that going back to Bethany was the last thing in the world I wanted to do. He probably thought I would run away and go back home. This is the same brother that dropped me at the missionary school in my childhood, and left me crying. Now he was taking me again, not to the elementary school, but to the orphanage.

The bus ride took about fifteen minutes. The distance was not long, but the bus made frequent stops. There were no official bus stops and anyone could get on or off at any time. Once more I begged my brother to let me go back home with him. He would not let me. Feelings of despair overwhelmed me. My own family was rejecting me. I craved for them and, at least on the surface, they did not care. Seven or eight years back, there was not much else I could do. Now, though I was only twelve, I realized there were some other things I could do besides cry.

I had never seen a movie in my life. I had never been to the cinema, nor watched television, nor listened to the radio. My world revolved around the convent and my school. I lacked the imagination to plan anything, and I lacked everything else, including money. What chances did I have?

Deep inside I did not want to continue to live this resigned and defeated life. I was dying a slow death every day. Come what may, I decided to put a stop to this. I only wished my brother would trust me to climb up the steep hill leading to the convent alone. It would save him precious time. It would also save him having to wait for another bus and pay another ticket. So I put on a serious face and pretended I was ready to go back to my lonely, miserable life.

It worked. My brother bought into my trick. As soon as the bus arrived at the bottom of the hill that led to the convent, my brother rang the bell for the driver to stop. I smiled, kissed my brother goodbye and got off. I started walking uphill and waited expectantly to hear the bus rumble off in the distance. I did not even turn my face to wave to my brother. As soon as the noise of the engine died in my ears, I looked back and there was no one. The bus had disappeared, and my brother with it. For the first time, I felt free. I was too far from the convent for anyone to see me. My brother was gone. He would not be back home until evening.

This was the start of another adventure. This is when another page of my life story began to be written. I turned around and started walking back to Jerusalem, certain that I could remember the location of the room where my family lived. For a good number of years, I had walked the road between Bethany and the old city, on my way to school and back to the convent. But this time it was a one-way trip—I was headed home. I had decided that nothing and no one would ever send me away again. I wanted to be home. I wanted to belong. I craved a family of my own.

The trip took about an hour. I was half running, but my mind was racing. I needed a believable story to tell my brothers. I also needed some good answers to the challenges they would present against my arguments to live with them. And yet, my need for time to cook up a story was not as strong as my desire to get home, as soon as possible. I could taste the flavor of family life, of a place I could call home, even if it were only a single room.

Finally, I arrived—but to my dismay, no one was there! Their words explaining that they could not keep me company came home to me. What is a home without family, but brick and concrete? I was not interested in where they lived or in what they had, as little as it was. All I wanted was them. But they were not there. I sat by the doorway and waited. I was hungry. I was tired. Nonetheless, I was happy. Yes, a little apprehensive, but happy.

Before long, my brother Joseph showed up. He was surprised and anguished—happy to see me, but troubled by the prospect of handling my inconvenient presence. When he asked why I was there, I told him a very unconvincing tale of being shot at by someone as I was walking up the hill to go to the convent.

He knew I was lying, and I was not surprised. If I were in his shoes, I don't think I would have believed such a flimsy tale either. I had tried on my way home that afternoon to come up with a more credible story. I had considered telling him that the iron gate to the orphanage was latched closed, but I was even less convinced they would buy that. What I lacked in imagination, however, I made up for with drama. Not that I was any better at that, but at least I could rely on my tears to soften my brother's heart. I hoped my tears would intercede for me.

I could see in his eyes that Joseph loved me. He was not angry, just helpless. He knew they could not afford another mouth to feed, another body to dress; nor did they have time to devote to caring and nurturing a younger brother. His reasoning was pragmatic and sound, but I didn't want to hear reasoning. He spanked my buttocks softly. I sensed he was venting off his frustration, not so much with me, but with himself. It was his way of trying to reconcile his heart with his mind. I knew this is where the battle was. In the end, his heart overpowered his mind, and he allowed me to stay. To me that was one first big battle won!

The debate and pleading were reenacted once more when

Salem arrived at home. This time, however, I quietly hung back and let Joseph play the role of advocate on my behalf. I had exhausted my talent for drama in persuading Joseph that he should let me stay, and now it was up to him, skeptical though he was of my story, to soften Salem's heart. Clearly, my tears, my pleading for a chance to live with a family of my own, convinced Joseph to give me a chance, because in the end he was convinced enough to tell Salem to give his blessing too.

As I look back at the events of that day, nearly fifty years ago, I have no doubt it was not my claims of being able to care for myself that made them accept my pleas. It was their love, a love that manifests itself between us to this day. At that time, I did not quite know yet the extent of our family's poverty and how they were struggling to get by each day. They, however, did know how difficult it would be to make space for a third body in that one room, but they accepted that sacrifice. When I look back on their willingness to accept even more hardship in their lives for me, I am as grateful today as I was on that day when they passed their verdict in my favor and welcomed me into my new home.

The next day, when my father came home to check on his sons, as he would do every two or three days, he was dismayed to find a third son in that small room they called home. He created quite a ruckus, and insisted that my presence was too great of a burden for my family to bear. My father was 55 years older than I. He could have easily been my grandfather. I could not possibly argue with him. I didn't really know him. I had seen him on occasion, but I had not lived with him prior to this summer. I did not know how far I could go or what to expect of him. His arguments were convincing, but not quite enough! I was good at school. He had seen my medallions. I said that I was as good at house chores. That was true. In Bethany, they made us do all types of work. I was used to cleaning, mopping, dusting, washing dishes, and even washing clothes. He kept repeating that he would have to remarry if I were to stay home, and marriage was one thing he had tried once and failed at. He did not want to repeat that. Nevertheless, there was no one to care for his youngest son, and he could not just walk away from that problem.

Even then, though my overwhelming concern was that I not be sent back to the orphanage, I felt sorry for my father. I did not like to see him in this predicament, especially when I was the cause of it. I felt sorry for my brothers too. I had no idea how much, or rather how little, money my father earned, but I could tell that the three of them were barely making it.

2

Life Outside the Box

BEING a tourist city, Jerusalem offered the means to making a living to anyone who knew a foreign language. In that I had an edge or two over my brothers. The public school they attended provided education in the Arabic language only. My annual scholarship at the private French school topped that with two more: English and French.

I sought to put that to good use. I knew Jerusalem well. I could walk it almost blindfolded. Guiding a tourist here or there and selling souvenirs at a tourist shop after school hours were always welcome. So at age fourteen I started earning my own money. It was not much, but anything was welcome. Even if no one else used it but me, at least I was not adding to my family's burdens.

Months later my father remarried. His wife, Rose, was Jordanian, a different culture from ours. This time there were pictures, wedding pictures. The world had changed considerably between my dad's first marriage and his second. Or maybe my father had changed.

At first I refused to believe that my dad would have to remarry if I decided to stay home. I did not want him to remarry for me. I was old enough to do the household chores; I had done them at the orphanage. Yet I have to admit that once he did, there was a very noticeable difference in our daily life now that a woman was running the house.

There was also quite a bit of adjustment needed on both sides. My brothers had been running the show for some years. Between them and my dad it was a male-dominated home. Now a woman had invaded their world and mine.

The adjustment for my stepmother was significant as well. With absolutely no previous experience, she was expected to care for male teenagers—not just one, but three! And on top of that, she had to share a single room with all of us. Yet Rose was gracious and graceful. Though no one set any boundaries, she set her own, and never once forced her way or her opinion. I was especially blessed to have a mother figure in her.

Soon after, a fourth brother joined the fold. Abe, the brother I had seen in a black robe years before, had been a boarding student at a Jesuit seminary. But after six or seven years of training, and with just one more year of theological education before graduation, he decided to quit. Celibacy was not for him. There was nowhere else to go but home.

Suddenly, we had a full house—a really full house. We were four brothers, my sixty-eight-year-old father and his wife, all living in one room. It was barely one year into my father's remarriage when his wife gave birth to an adorable baby girl, Reem, who soon became the center of everyone's attention. No one gave much thought to the ever-increasing crowdedness in that one room. No one spoke of sending anyone away anymore. My sense of family was slowly, but firmly, being restored.

A second baby girl, Suzan, arrived before long. By that time, we had moved into a larger apartment in a different part of town—the Jewish quarter of the old city of Jerusalem. My father, his wife and the two girls had one bedroom to themselves, while my brothers and I shared the other bedroom. On the surface, the only thing our move accomplished was to provide more room for everyone. Yet a number of events occurred at the new place that would shape my life forever.

My older brother Josef began attending the University of Damascus in Syria. Though a full-time student, he was in a program in which he would go for a few weeks at a time. He was a good student and a hard worker, and did well. It was not surprising, since he had also excelled in the public high school in Jerusalem, graduating seventh nationwide. Years later under Jordanian rule he would become the General Superintendent of the Income Tax Department for the West Bank.

It was not long before my immediate older brother, Salem, also went to university, in Egypt, to study medicine. He received a full scholarship: Everything was provided, including the ticket to get there. He had done exceedingly well in his final year in high school, even better than Joseph, coming out fifth nationwide. I belonged to a family of geniuses, and I did not know it!

Prior to going to Egypt, Salem approached me one day and asked if I would accept a copy of the New Testament. I had no clue what he meant by that. *What does Testament mean, and what did the New Testament refer to?* Though I had attended a Catholic school and had lived at a Catholic orphanage, I was completely ignorant of what the New Testament was or what it contained between its covers.

Once I realized what Salem was offering me, I was indignant, despite my ignorance. How could he propose that to me? He had gone to a Muslim public school all his life. I had gone to a Christian Catholic school. Who did he think he was?

When I asked him where he got his New Testament, he said that he had been going to a Baptist church. Salem had become Protestant—and so had Joseph! My indignation turned to fury. My brothers had become heretics, and were pressuring me to follow suit. I figured their New Testament was probably a forged Protestant copy of the original, exclusively Catholic, edition. There was absolutely nothing on earth that could convince me to accept his book.

Weeks, probably months went by, and I held the same bigoted attitude. My curiosity finally overpowered my indignation, however; I swallowed my pride, took the New Testament and began reading it in private. I was awed by what I read. By the time I fell asleep that evening, I had covered the first sixteen chapters of the book of Mathew. Within a week, I completed the entire New Testament for the first time.

This was a miracle book, out of the ordinary in every respect. It demanded one's admiration, one's amazement, but most notably, one's faith. I knew the baby Jesus who was laid in a manger in Bethlehem. Little did I know of the other Jesus; the Jesus that spoke so profoundly, the Jesus that silenced His enemies, the Jesus that raised Lazarus, or the Jesus that claimed divinity. If the New Testament demanded my faith, the Jesus of the New Testament demanded my worship. He alone deserved it.

Soon my amazement turned into perplexity, and my perplexity to discontentment. If this was God's Word, why had my church never given it to me? That book raised serious questions in my mind, questions about faith and doctrine.

I was brought up Catholic and was proud of it. The Sisters of Charity were role models living out the love of Christ very sacrificially. Some had left their countries and were living as missionaries to serve us at the orphanage. The Catholic monks that ran the day school I attended in downtown Jerusalem were above reproach. They were not preachers, but they lived out in practice the longsuffering and kindness that Christ spoke of in the New Testament. Some things made sense, while others did not. I decided to check things out for myself.

There was no purgatory in the Protestant New Testament (unless, I reasoned, the Protestants omitted it). There was no Mary worship, and no Mass (unless they omitted those too). A score of other elements of faith and doctrine screamed in my face. The Protestant church could not have taken all those elements away and replaced them by putting different words in the mouth of Christ. They could not have stolen Paul's pen to rewrite his epistles. That would be forgery! We were taught that Protestants were heretics, and we believed that, but no one said they had forged the Bible! I wondered how the Catholic New Testament would compare. But I had no access to one in the early 1960s.

A battle was raging deep within me, and I could not win it on my own. I needed help. As a good Catholic, my first priority was to defend my faith; to defend what I believed in. I didn't claim to know my Catholic faith well. But I thought that after many years at the orphanage and at my

Catholic school, I had a good enough understanding of it. Now it was being undermined, and not by people, but by a Book.

I could not help but notice what appeared to be a huge divergence between the things I was made to believe and what the New Testament seemed to teach. Deep down I wanted some clues on how to reconcile the two. Surely my school teachers, mostly Catholic monks, well-trained in the faith, would be able to quench my thirsty soul. Help was abundantly available, or so I thought.

What was lacking was boldness to ask my questions. I was not sure what my teachers would think of me if I raised these issues. My image as a good Catholic was extremely important to me. My reputation as a student was unblemished. I did not want my spiritual quest to be tarnished either.

Once again, curiosity overpowered my fears and concern for my image. One day after class, I summed up every iota of courage and went to my teacher of catechism, Brother Philippe. Brother Philippe not only taught catechism, he lived it. He was kind and patient. He never raised his voice in class. I felt it was safe to go to him.

I assumed that I had done something against Catholic practice in accepting a copy of the Protestant New Testament, and worse yet, actually reading it. I also assumed that if Catholics were allowed to have their own copy, I would have had mine a long time ago. I spent the night thinking of the best way to ask my questions without raising any doubts in the mind of Brother Philippe. I hoped that my cleverly composed questions would assure him that I was as much Catholic after reading that book as I was before, even more so. I needed his help to effectively defend my faith, and hopefully win my brothers back into the fold. (I took the coward's way out and hid the battle that was raging within me.)

I knocked on his door. He invited me in, sat me before him and gently asked what he could do for me. I felt at ease. I asked him about purgatory, and where the New Testament spoke of it. I added that my intention was to convince my brothers of the validity of *our* Catholic doctrine. I had gone over that question so many times in my head I thought I could say it flawlessly.

Perhaps my facial expression betrayed me, or I had simply stumbled into dangerous territory, but I had barely finished asking the question when his facial expression changed. Seconds before, sitting at his desk was a composed, even-tempered gentleman. Now I was facing a very different person.

I had run to him seeking refuge from my confusion. I had hoped he would come to my side, place his warm hand over me, and endow me with a portion of his tranquility and composure. Instead, he frowned, rose from his desk, pointed his finger at me and thundered, "Who is it that gave you this book, and how did you allow yourself to read it?"

I thought I was the one with questions, but apparently I was wrong! I was not prepared for this. His questions, or rather his *questioning*, was unrelenting. He was not about to let this go without getting to the bottom of things.

I was at a loss as to what to do or say. After all, Brother Philippe had the authority to do what he pleased. I was completely at his mercy. He could, for example, revoke my scholarship. (We were too poor to afford my tuition at this private school, and at the end of every school year my father would make a plea to extend my scholarship. My grades helped my father make a better case, but the final decision was made by the school.)

Cowed in my chair in Brother Philippe's office that afternoon, I wondered if my school days were over. I could imagine myself being thrown out—expelled. I was fifteen, with two or three more years of school ahead of me. What a shame it would be if, after all these years, I was not able to graduate—and all because I asked one naive question!

In reality, it was not the question that was naive. I was. But there was no giving in. I had not made that discovery for nothing. To me the issue was not about the Catholic and the Protestant churches. It was about my life. I was not only naive—I was stubborn.

I spent many weeks in mental anguish, searching for the truth, but in many ways limiting my search to only one direction. I refused to believe that I had followed the teachings of men all these years. It was impossible to think that Sister Agnes was wrong. She was good, and I figured that truth had to be related to goodness.

And yet, I still had questions—objective questions about faith and doctrine, which could only be resolved objectively. It seemed like I was in a dark tunnel and didn't know which way to go. But though surrounded by darkness, there was light inside my mind! The reading of the New Testament had lit something within me—a light that no one could challenge.

Thankfully, I was not thrown out of school, though Brother Philippe's attitude toward me, both inside and outside the classroom, would never be the same again.

After months of hesitation, I decided to attend the Baptist church, just to check them out. Who were they? What else beside the Bible did they believe in? Who was their big leader, their Pope? What kind of following did they have? If they were on the side of the truth, surely they had huge numbers of followers like my brothers Joseph and Salem. I intended to find out for myself.

At every juncture, whether accepting for the first time that copy of the New Testament, asking my school teacher that naive question, or now stepping out of my comfort zone to attend the Baptist church, my curiosity seemed to always overpower my hesitation. But it was only after many months that I finally attended the church—reluctantly, hiding behind my brother Joseph. I did not want to answer any intrusive questions from anyone I did not know.

My first visit to the Baptist Church in East Jerusalem took as much courage as my talk with Brother Philippe. I did not want to deny my Catholic faith, and going to this church seemed like a big step in that direction. What if one of my friends or classmates saw me go there, and spread it around my school? How would Brother Philippe react then?

My first impression was nothing short of shock. I honestly wondered how they dared call their place of worship a church. This group of people met in the basement of an office building just outside Herod's Gate. If the place was pathetic, their number was much more so. The church was made up of less than a dozen individuals, many of whom were not even from our city. If they owned the truth as they claimed they did, how come there were so few of them, and no one else seemed to bother? My foundations were being tested again.

Nonetheless, I went and kept going week after week. I heard preaching from the Bible—in Arabic—like I never heard before. It was there that I first learned of grace, of faith, of evangelism, and of inviting others to follow Jesus. Having read the New Testament in its entirety helped me understand much of the background. It made a lot of sense. Yet, in the back of my mind, I told myself I did not need all that. I was already a Christian, *un bon enfant*! A good boy!

Soon after, because I knew English, I was asked to interpret for American preachers who came to visit, and translate the soundtracks for Christian films. I had an ear for music, so it was not long before the church offered to pay for a blind teacher to give me private lessons. My musical "ear" kept getting in the way, however; I never took enough time to read the notes or practice as I should. Despite that, the group was gracious enough to invite me to play, especially since no one else could do it better. All of that underlined, rightly or wrongly, my perception of myself. I was good—religiously good.

At the tender age of seventeen, I had already been through a number of major upheavals and changes, and with each one my life took a new turn. For most of my first thirteen years of life, I was sheltered within the confines of a Catholic orphanage in Bethany. At age seventeen my world was very different—and much bigger—than it had been.

After running away to my father's house, nothing seemed constant. From the Christian Quarter where he and two of my older brothers lived, we moved to a bigger apartment in the Jewish Quarter. It seemed that each new change, each new encounter, was only a means to prepare me for what was still to come. For months we had lived crammed, six of us, in one room. Now in the Jewish Quarter, we could finally afford some space for my older sister Marie to also leave the Catholic girls convent and live with us.

By contrast with the Christian Quarter, where mostly Christians lived, the Jewish Quarter was largely inhabited by Muslims, not Jews or Christians, though we were not the only Christian family there. Our landlady was a devout Muslim. I became friends with Ahmad, her grandson.

I liked Ahmad. We had a lot in common. We were the same age and in the same grade, although he went to a public school, while I continued attending the private Catholic school. We both liked pool. It was not long before we became good friends.

During the first few months of my friendship with Ahmad, we did not discuss religion. I had very little understanding of the Muslim faith, even though Ahmad was not the first Muslim boy I befriended. I had had quite a few Muslim classmates at school, but at the time it seemed to me that everyone attending my school was Catholic. I had no clue as to how we differed, and paid little or no attention to the matter. We all worshiped "Allah"; this is how we all, without exception, identified deity in our Arabic language. That was all about to change—or to put it another way, I was about to change.

Ahmad was Muslim before we became friends. He was Muslim after we became friends. But I changed. I had come across a most marvelous book, and I wanted to share the insights I had gained from it with him. As we played ball in our street one day I approached Ahmad with a question that threw him off guard. I asked him if he would be interested in reading the New Testament. He was silent for a minute. "Let me ask my parents," he said.

I have to admit that I knew what his parents would say. I knew they would tell Ahmad to decline my offer. What I didn't know was what else they would tell him. Ahmad was forbidden to talk with me. Our relationship was terminated.

I had acted out of ignorance; possibly out of a good heart, but still out of ignorance. I was making a religious statement, and that did not sit well with his parents. Our friendship was aborted before it could mature. I was suddenly drawn into the world of adult thinking and behavior. Organized religion has this magical power within it that shapes people's identities. Regretfully, it can erect walls and build fences, like it did that day between Ahmad and me.

Often I have thought of this early friendship, and the direct effects of organized religion on me, even in my childhood. I miss Ahmad, even today. He was a good boy. But my religion got in the way and ruined everything. I wish I could see him again, though I don't know what I would say or do. Possibly I would just give him a hug and tell him that I missed him.

This was now my last year at De La Salle Frères College in Jerusalem. During my last three years of high school, one more major change occurred in my life—a change that overshadowed all the previous ones put together! I stopped going to Mass and began attending the Baptist church. My faith in catechism was at its lowest. I was a strong believer in the Bible. I was gradually becoming indoctrinated in the Baptist way of interpreting Scripture and the world.

I also learned how to play table tennis. I became so good at it that I won the school's championship that year. I also learned to play pool, and began going to bars and sport clubs in town spending whatever money I could get my hands on to be able to play. I even secretly emptied my father's pockets of his coins. It was not long before I was caught redhanded and severely reprimanded. My dad never spanked me. His reprimands were enough. He was fifty-five years my senior. His looks were enough to send me trembling. I was also beginning to like girls.

My grades were soon affected. I lost my *Prix d'Excellence*. For the last three years I barely received the *Prix d'Honneur* (no medallion was awarded with that; it just meant I was one of the top three students). I had always been good in sciences, especially mathematics. I earned an excellent reputation, and prided myself on how, after each math exam, my classmates would come to me and check out their answers. Upon graduation, the Governor of Jerusalem handed me my math prize. I had finished first.

My dream was to pursue an education in math. My school promised a full scholarship at Loyola University in the USA. All my past hardships were finally coming to an end. The world could not contain my joy. It was only a matter of time, and I would be free as a bird. My application process seemed to go well. I was told to check with Nawwas Travels, just outside the Damascus Gate. My student visa would be sent to their office, and they would issue my tickets. I waited impatiently!

3

Two Eventful Encounters

I WAS leaving for America after graduation at the end of
June, so I had no time to waste, especially if I was going
to say goodbye to my friends and family. My sister Marie
had married her cousin and was now living with her in-laws
(my mother's only sister) in the land of our birthplace, some
40 miles to the north of Jerusalem. I had been there a couple
of times after I had left the Catholic orphanage in Bethany.
The house was in the countryside, and it was beautiful. My
aunt and her family had vineyards, and many other fruit
trees. I enjoyed those visits, though few and far between.
They always seemed very brief. But this time it was different.

I arrived at the house in the late morning. It consisted of
a small courtyard encircled by four main rooms—one for
my sister and her husband (my cousin), one for my aunt
and her unmarried daughters, one for my single male cousins, and one for the cattle. My sister was out, but my aunt
was home. As was customary when greeting older relatives

and acquaintances, I bent over and kissed the back of her right hand. (This is a sign of respect, and carries with it a sense of asking for their approval and blessing.) My aunt responded by kissing me on both cheeks. Despite her years, she was beautiful, with very smooth skin—probably the good effects of using the oil from her family's olive orchard. It brought back memories of my mother, her younger sister— if she were still alive, she would probably look like my aunt, only more beautiful.

I had barely taken a seat and begun to enjoy the cool of their stone house when there was knock on the metal gate. My aunt rushed to open it. A woman passed into the court-yard and entered with my aunt into the kitchen/living room where I sat waiting.

The woman who appeared in the door wore an excep-tionally long dress with long sleeves, despite the heat of the summer, and her head was covered. My aunt invited her to come in, calling her Om Ahmad. (A married woman is ad-dressed by the term *Om*—Arabic for "mother of"—followed by the name of her firstborn son. And if she does not have a son, she is still addressed with that term, but the son's name is replaced by the name of her husband's father.)

The name my aunt used caught my attention: *Om Ahmad*—Mother of Ahmad! She was a Muslim! Ahmad was the name of the Jerusalem friend I had lost with my reli-gious zeal—and my ignorance. I promised myself never to make the same mistake again.

In Middle Eastern culture, men are not supposed to gaze at women. And women, especially if married, are not sup-posed to look into men's eyes. But as I rose to shake her hand, I allowed myself to steal a glance at her face. I was only eighteen; more a boy than a man. Om Ahmad appeared to be in her late forties, possibly older. She stretched out her hand and gave me a brief, formal and emotionless handshake.

Suddenly, my aunt froze. She turned to look at her guest, as if seeing her for the first time. Then she looked at me. Her perennial smile had vanished. Her blue eyes seemed to penetrate me, but her mind was elsewhere. Apparently she had something important to say—more important than fetching a glass of cold water for her guest. But why these strangely serious looks?

With her eyes transfixed on us, my aunt asked her guest if she knew who I was. This time the woman looked at me again—or rather, stared at me. I could tell from her expression that she didn't know me, any more than I knew her. She shook her head, as much in disbelief at the question as to say no.

But my aunt would not give up. She briskly turned her attention to me and asked if I knew who this woman was! I thought to myself, *How many times have I been to your home? How on earth would you expect me to know a woman whom I've just set my eyes on for the first time in my life?*

The truth is, my aunt was not expecting us to know each other. Her mind had raced back to something in the past which she was about to reveal, and she wanted to create the most impact. She definitely got our attention—all of it! She was dying to say something; and we were dying to hear it.

A moment or two of silence passed. Her serious look disappeared as suddenly as it came, and with a twinkle in her eye and a grin on her face, she said to me, "Hanna, this is the

woman who nursed you when your mother was dying of
cancer." To the woman she said, "This is my sister Wadia's
baby that you breast-fed."

We both froze in shock. My aunt's plan to make a dra-
matic announcement had totally succeeded—but I don't
think she had thought about how we would react. What
were we supposed to do? What was *I* supposed to do?

As it was, I did not have to do anything. Om Ahmad
turned and took a step toward me. I looked into her eyes;
they were filled with tears. She didn't say a word, but threw
her arms around my slim shoulders and began to cry uncontrollably, showering my cheeks with kisses. Did she sense
that she had found a son? Perhaps she was childless, and saw
me as the son she had always dreamed of having!

Women's tears are powerful; even those of a total stranger
can be magically effectual. Om Ahmad's tears were no exception. In this emotionally charged moment, the sad fact
of my mother's death and the loving embrace of Om Ahmad
brought tears to my own eyes. For an instant I thought of
my years in the orphanage and wondered why my family
did not allow Om Ahmad to raise me as her own. It would
have saved me the molestation, the solitude, the deprivation. It would have blessed her life with the child she had
always desired.

I had found a mother—a *Muslim* mother! Here I was a
Christian, the descendant of long generations of Christians,
bearing a very Christian name, yet having been nursed by a
Muslim woman! I did not know how to react to this or make
sense of it. Not that I was ungrateful—it was just that the
meaning of it all eluded me! What was I to do now?

For a moment, religious differences became utterly meaningless. And for perhaps the first time, I began to ask myself, *Who created religions to begin with?* It could not be God. Otherwise He would have created one religion—His religion—not dozens. And who invented barriers between religions? It could not be God either. The plurality of religions presupposed barriers of all sorts between them. If that is not the work of God, it must be the work of man, or some other divisive, evil power.

An awesome feeling of indebtedness overwhelmed me. I owed my life, in part at least, to this woman—a person of another faith. How could I ever repay her? How could I repay her people? That, in essence, became my obsession.

There have been very few times in my life when my tears literally choked me and I was unable to speak. This was one of them. I stood there and cried; Om Ahmad cried; my aunt cried. This is not why I had come from Jerusalem; I had simply wanted to say goodbye before pursuing my education in the USA. But that chance encounter with my nursing mother changed my life forever!

I planned my visit to be a short one, but my sister Marie, the closest to me after my brother Salem, pleaded with me to stay longer. I knew she would begin crying the minute I told her I was preparing to leave. She would then go out of her way to make me the foods I liked, all the while begging me to stay just one more day.

Marie craved for family like I did. She also had lived the best part of her childhood at a convent, and orphanage for girls. She was probably sent there at about the same time I was sent away, and with the same lame excuse. I did not want to hurt her feelings; it was painful for me as well, especially when I did not know whether or when we would meet again. But I had to go.

Now back in Jerusalem after that eventful encounter, I could not wait to check with the travel agent about my visa. I had been there so many times that they had told me not to bother to come anymore. They said they would notify me as soon as my visa was received. But I figured I had a good excuse: I had been out of town and they could not have reached me. Besides, they couldn't contact me anyway—I didn't have a telephone!

So here I was at their door asking again, and receiving the same answer for the umpteenth time: The visa had not arrived. I began to lose hope. Although I had been promised a scholarship, the student visa never came, and in September of 1966, I was still in Jerusalem. My dream to go to the USA vanished. I did not want to go to an Arab university, yet even if I did want to, I had done all my education in French and English, while most Arab universities taught in Arabic. There were some private universities, like the American University in Beirut. But that was way above our means. I was stuck.

Completely against my wishes, I began attending an Arab college in Jerusalem. To me, it seemed like a waste of time; I was learning many of the same things over again. I had prided myself on the education I received at the French private school, and now my pride was being crushed. I would have to settle for an Arab university somewhere. Even that was not a given. First I would have to pass a country-wide entrance exam, and I had neither the confidence or desire to do it.

Since I had been going to the Baptist church for about two years and was considered one of the group, I was able to land a job at the Baptist bookstore, located right above the basement where we conducted our church services. If nothing else, working at the store improved my spoken English and French, as I came into continuous contact with tourists. I started there full time, but a few months later, another church member was hired to run the store, and I continued as a part-timer. I supplemented my income by selling souvenirs in the streets of the old city, just as I had done when I was younger.

Sometime in late 1966 or early 1967, our church invited the late Rev. Zomot from Jordan to be our revival speaker for the whole week. Our pastor challenged us to invite guests. I forget if I succeeded in inviting anyone. But I know I was there every evening.

Our regular Sunday services were usually attended by the members, roughly a dozen people or less. The hall could hold eight or ten times that number. Midweek services, whether for prayer or otherwise, had even poorer attendance. That may have been one reason why our pastors did not seem to stay too long. In the two years that I had been going, several pastors had come and gone. That probably also explains the special meetings that the Jordanian pastor was invited to conduct. The church would be filled, even if only temporarily.

And filled it was! I had never seen so many people in our little church. Unfortunately, most of the visitors were members of other Protestant churches from out of town. Try as we might, we had failed to convince strangers to come.

Unlike other Palestinian cities and towns, Jerusalem had an excess of churches, and most of its members probably had the religious self-satisfaction that I had. I had grown up here, and like everyone else I prided myself on our great cathedrals. Why would anyone leave the Church of the Holy Sepulchre or some other grand edifice to worship in our basement?

For years I had joined thousands of other Christians, both locals and pilgrims, in the Palm Sunday procession. Carrying palm branches, we would walk from the Mount of Olives down through the Kidron Valley, stopping at Gethsemane before arriving at the *Via Dolorosa*. In one voice the city could hear the chanting of this huge throng: *Hosanna in the highest!* Our last station always ended at the Church of the Holy Sepulchre.

Numerous times I attended the "miracle of light" that used to take place at that church six days after Palm Sunday. Multitudes would begin to assemble early in the afternoon to make sure they had a good spot inside the church; others crowded the entrance between the huge columns. There were no lights anywhere to be seen, either inside or out, not until the miracle took place. The smell of perfume and incense filled our nostrils, while chanting filled the air. Each of us carried one or more candles and waited in the dark.

We waited for the priest to come out of the tomb where Jesus is believed to have been laid two thousand years ago. The priest usually came out at exactly midnight, the night before Jesus was to be raised from the dead. He came out carrying the flame of light and life, and he would pass it on until it reached everyone. I would then do my best to keep the little flicker going until I reached my father's house. Like the church, my father's house would be kept in the dark all night until the lit candle arrived.

In my heart I could not blame those who had turned

down invitations to the revival meetings. I had been just like them. I was much like them even now. It was true that during the past two years I had learned much of the New Testament faith and doctrine, and prided myself on having read the Bible from cover to cover a couple of times. But I had not changed much beyond that. To begin with, I didn't sense any need to change, even in the revival meetings, and certainly not with our guest speaker's choice of Bible passages. Like those strangers who had turned down our invitations, I felt I was religiously good, and I was from the holy city of Jerusalem. In my ignorance and zeal I even tried to turn Ahmad the Muslim into a Christian. I knew I was not perfect. But who was? I was as close as one could get.

The week-long revival meetings began at 6 or 7 pm. As I joined the congregation and settled in the pew to listen, I thought to myself that I had heard much better preachers during the two years I had been coming to this church. It was now Wednesday, the third evening of the revival meetings, and so far this man, Rev. Zomot, had preached only from very well-known passages of Scripture. Tonight the passage he had selected was also familiar, even boringly so: Matthew 7, the Sermon on the Mount. He spoke on the narrow and wide gates.

I wondered what new elements this preacher was going to uncover in his message. Would he preach something the passage does not say, just to make it sound fresh and new? It would be hard to do in this case, since the language and imagery Jesus used was so simple and straightforward a child could understand it.

I sat puzzled, wondering whether our church pastor was having second thoughts about our revival speaker; I knew I had. *No wonder no one was getting saved! No wonder no one shouted Hallelujah or Amen!* I wasn't shouting, and definitely didn't plan to. But I sat through the message nonetheless.

As he had done the two preceding nights, the preacher ended his message and asked that we close our eyes and bow our heads for prayer. I was used to this pattern; it was how our pastor always ended his messages, and nothing ever seemed to happen after that. Why should this night be any different?

No sooner had I closed my eyes and bowed down my head than a strange feeling overcame my soul. My life was being displayed like a film before me. For the first time I saw the ugliness of my soul. I lusted; I stole; I lied. I did many other things—things I covered up with my religiosity! Suddenly I was not the *bon enfant* anymore. I stood naked before God, and I knew it. My sinfulness was screaming in my face. I was not walking the narrow road. I was on my way to perdition. I was under the judgment of sin and death. I could not remain in my seat, even with my head bowed down. I wanted to go flat on my face. Instead, I went down on my knees while my tears ran down my cheeks.

The facts I knew too well. They had not changed. I had read them and reread them. I had heard them being preached time and again. It was not the doctrine of salvation by faith that convicted me of my sin. It was not the doctrine of the Trinity, or any other doctrine for that matter. I had an encounter with my sinfulness and the agent was God's Spirit. Through my tears, I prayed. I lifted up my soul to God and asked for His forgiveness. Jesus had paid my penalty through His death on the cross of Golgotha. A heavy burden was lifted off. Joy welled up in my soul. Something had happened within me. It was instantaneous. It was magnificent. It was indescribable, but it wasn't man-made. And it had nothing to do with doctrine—Catholic or Protestant!

As I walked home that evening, feelings of elation, of newness, of sheer ecstasy ran through me like a flowing river. Everything around me seemed new. I had walked those streets hundreds of times before. The old city of Jerusalem had not changed. I had. For several nights in a row, I would see myself walking on thin air, almost flying. A new and exciting chapter was being written in my life, and I was not the author.

4

Bartering with God

MY SCHOOL year at the Arab college was almost over. I had gone there in an attempt to salvage my education at the French private school, and pave the way to go to an Arab university, since my dream of education in the USA had fallen through. During the last few months, I was more interested in talking about Christ to my classmates than doing my homework. I was filling my school bag with copies of the New Testament and other Christian material rather than my school books.

At the French school I was always envied for my distinction in math, bookkeeping and chemistry, to name but a few subjects. But that was all in the past. During this year, I attempted to learn the Arabic symbols for the chemical elements, but I was not confident I could pass the chemistry exam. My biggest nightmare, though, was math. I had embarrassed myself a number of times in class asking and re-asking questions, trying to understand calculus, but to no avail. My brain was trained to compute in one language, and it was not Arabic. My chances of ever becoming an engineer were gradually but surely going up in smoke.

Two weeks before the start of the finals, Egyptian President Gamal Abdel Nasser ordered UN troops out of the Sinai, then closed the Strait of Tiran to Israeli navigation. Much drum-beating was going on. Those days were very tense.

I was also very tense on June 5, 1967, but for a different reason: I was sitting at my desk during the final exam in math, trying to decipher the calculus problems staring up at me. Half an hour had barely passed when the supervisor entered the room and ordered everyone to go home. The war had started—the Six-Day War!

Nervousness was quickly replaced by fear. My calculus exam was now behind me. All I wanted to do was to get home as quickly as possible. Since our family had moved to a newer apartment outside the city walls, facing Mount Hadassah, I now had to walk the better part of two miles. If we had still lived in our old apartment, it would have taken me three short minutes to be home.

The location of the apartment mattered, but not much. Western Jerusalem, the Jewish part of town, was close by wherever you lived—inside or outside the old city walls. Our national enemy, Israel, was literally next door. There was barbed wire between us, nothing more. For a second I wished we were still living inside the city walls, where the streets are narrow and intertwined, and where people could move a little more freely without being noticed.

Our new apartment was on a main artery. Facing us was a Jewish settlement, sitting atop the hill in the distance. Part of an arrangement brokered by the UN allowed the continued existence of this Jewish settlement on Arab Palestinian soil after Jerusalem was partitioned in 1948.

UN armored vehicles provided safe passage of a Jewish convoy that crossed through the Mandelbaum Gate from Western Jerusalem into Eastern Jerusalem all the way to Mount Hadassah. No one from the general public knew what went on in that settlement; no Arab was allowed anywhere near it. Living right across from it gave us a creepy feeling, and all the more now that the war had been declared.

For about a month or so before June 5, we were watching Jordanian troop movements in *Wadi El Jaws* (Arabic for "Valley of Walnut Trees") across from our balcony. That army base was a couple of hundred yards away, midway between our neighborhood and the Jewish settlement on Mount Hadassah.

At first, the sight of these troops was reassuring. Not anymore. Their presence in the middle of this peaceful neighborhood was an invitation for trouble—an end to peace.

I was the last in my family to make it home, at almost five in the afternoon. Everyone had been concerned for my safety. My father had the radio on. We all huddled around him to listen to the latest updates. *Sout El Arab* (Arabic for "Voice of the Arabs") was declaring that Egyptian batteries had downed forty Israeli jets. Then fifty! Then sixty! Within a couple of hours, they claimed that 120 Israeli jets had been shot down. Victory was on the horizon.

The Arab armies had been defeated in 1948. I had heard that from my father and read it in the Arabic history books. This new war was about saving face. My year at the Arab college had infused me with strong Arab sentiments. Like every other good Arab, I wanted us to win that war.

Soon it was dark, and every second of every minute counted. The power was out. Fear crept in. The local newscasts ordered everyone inside their homes. The situation had been scary, but with the night falling, it became terrifying. I went into one of the bedrooms and said a brief prayer. Well, not really a prayer—it was more like an attempt to make a deal with God. I had no assurance that He would accept my deal. But I had nothing to lose, and everything to gain. If only He would hear and accept the terms!

In my personal studies of the Old Testament, I had come across the shrewd, intriguing personality of Jacob. I was fascinated by him and learned some of his ways in making deals. He was a master wheeler-dealer, and he got what he asked for. Would God do the same for me?

I was just a few months old when the 1948 war took place, so this was a new experience for me. All I wanted was to be safe—and not just me, but everyone in our household. And we were quite a few: my father, my stepmother, my brother Joseph and my two stepsisters. My young niece, Vivi, was also there with us, visiting from Amman, Jordan. If God would keep everyone safe—everyone—I would serve Him the rest of my life. It was a make-or-break deal.

There was not a second of calm all night long. The jets were pounding all around. The smell of burning vehicles, and of burning flesh, filled our house and our nostrils. Artillery lit the night sky. My sisters cried, as did my niece. I was a big boy—nineteen—so I could not cry.

At about five the next morning, all fighting ceased. Not a single bullet was heard. Instead, we could hear the noise of heavy machinery rolling below our balcony. Initially we thought Iraqi troops had come to our rescue, and to the rescue of the Jordanian army. But then my father overheard one single word. *Kaduma!* "The Israelis are in," he said. They were on our street, rolling inside our town with their tanks. Their orders were to move forward—to advance!

Those were very tense moments filled with trembling. What now? We had obviously lost the war. All that talk on the Arab newscasts was unfounded. No wonder most Arab audiences had learned to turn to foreign radio services for news they could trust.

We all sat crouched in one corner. We lost our appetite to eat or drink; we were chewing on our fears. We had not had nightmares until then, since none of us had slept. But now we had nightmares we could not wake up from. They were walking nightmares with machine guns, invading our quiet world, and there was no running away.

My father was shaken. He was well into his seventies, and had seen it all many times before. He had been drafted in World War I, and saw firsthand the atrocities that war brought to the world at large, and to his own world. He also survived World War II, and later the 1948 war between the Arabs and the Jews. But it seemed one can never get used to the stresses of war. As a good father, he had very deep-seated and legitimate concerns for his family. Beside his wife, he had two sons, two daughters and one grandchild. He had far too many responsibilities and too little control over the events that were unfolding!

I was, if anything, even less in control. There was not much I could do. My father was scared. My stepmother was scared. My brother Joseph was scared. And I was just as scared. Yes, I had prayed. But I was scared nonetheless.

In my limited understanding, I never imagined that one

nightmare could flow into another. It was as if one lightless tunnel was leading into a darker one. The Israeli tanks had rolled in, and we were doubled over, sweating in fear. But the unimaginable was yet to come.

A few minutes after five a.m. there was strong, hard, incessant knocking on our wooden door. My father was quick to react. "Don't move," he said. "The Jews are at our doorstep."

From outside the door, the order came in Arabic. Arabic with an accent! "*Iftah! Iftah!*"—Arabic for open! There was no mistaking. My dad was correct. The Jews were at our very doorstep!

I stood up. My father yelled at me to sit down and keep quiet. Never had I disobeyed him before or since. But that minute I did. "If the Arab armies with all their might could not stand against them," I said sarcastically, "do you think your wooden door can?" Once again, my father ordered me down. I looked at him in utter disbelief and started walking toward the door.

The distance from our little room where we were huddled to the doorway could be measured in inches. A step or two was all I needed. And yet, within that short distance my mind was racing. My heart was throbbing like an Olympic runner's. I am not a physician to explain or even understand how fear and apprehension affect our heartbeat, but I know firsthand how it feels.

As I started making my way toward the door, my brother Joseph was moving toward a back exit. I placed my hand on the door knob, and consequently placed my life in the hands of God. Eternity seemed very close, and not in a bad sense. In fact, the hope of eternity was one key element that gave me the boldness to stand up, firmly take control of the situation and face the enemy head up and head on. I flung the door open.

No sooner had I done that, than two dozen guns were pointed at me. All over me! "Put your hands on your head!" I did. "Get your family all out in the stairwell." I felt partly relieved. I was not shot at. I was still alive and breathing. I started calling my family out. Everyone came out—everyone except Joseph! I kept calling. He kept hiding. Precious seconds passed, and still no Joseph. I began to despair. Where on earth was he? My forehead was covered with cold sweat, but I could not wipe it. My hands were still up in the air. After what seemed like eternity, Joseph appeared in the doorway. The soldiers cocked their guns. As in a choir, we all screamed with one voice, "Don't shoot!" Thankfully, they did not.

God must have heard my prayer. I had dictated the terms. It looked like He heard me and accepted the deal. For me, He had kept His part of my contract with Him. He kept everyone of my family safe. He drove the point home, literally! Real danger was at our doorstep. My brother was about to be killed. But God overruled. It was my turn to keep my part. I had said that I would serve Him for as long as I lived. Now it seemed I had two debts to repay. I was indebted to Om Ahmad, the Muslim woman who helped keep me alive at birth. I was also indebted to God, who kept me alive through the 1967 war. My future life would combine these two aspects.

I don't know if my brother Joseph had also prayed that prayer, or bargained with God the way I did. I will ask him the next time I see him. All I know is that he has faithfully served God ever since. Joseph pastors the local Baptist church in Bethlehem!

5

A Moment of Truth

T HE CONQUEST of Jerusalem by the Israeli Defense
Forces (IDF) presented us with new opportunities and
challenges. One grand opportunity for me was the newly
established American College in West Jerusalem, the Jewish
side of the city. With the city now united, I could possibly
attend. I did not have to travel to the USA to pursue an
education in English.

One unexpected blessing for us, as well as possibly hundreds of other Palestinian families, was the reunion with family members and friends that the 1948 war had separated.
The youngest of my dad's three sisters and her family lived
in Jaffa, a seaside resort city on the Mediterranean Sea. My
father had not seen them in years, possibly decades. Now
that there were no more borders or barbed wire, my father
could finally visit his sister, his nieces and his nephews. (My
father's brother-in-law, my aunt's husband, had died some
time before.) Though I cannot say I missed that side of the
family, since I was only a baby at the time of the 1948 war, I

was thrilled to have "new" members added to our family. It was overwhelming!

It was also overwhelming, on the other extreme, to accept the challenge of living side by side with our enemies, the Jews. Or more precisely, to be under their control! The national ego in me was very much alive. I was brought up an Arab. The Arabic language was my heritage. My ancestors had spoken Arabic for untold centuries. To the Arabs, the Jews were *the* enemies!

To my amazement, I discovered that the Baptists, with whom I identified myself, had also started missionary work among the Jewish people. Before we knew it, visitors from the church in West Jerusalem started popping up in our basement, the place of worship we called church next to Herod's Gate. Most of the visitors were Baptist missionaries from the USA and their families, and it was not hard to accept them in our midst. Their names and faces were new to us, but not what they were doing or why they were here. God had used the Baptist mission to bring new life and new hope into our household, beginning with my brothers Joseph and Salem, and then me. If anything, I was thankful for their dedication.

Weeks later, those same missionaries invited us to visit the Baptist village in Petah Tikva in Israel proper. It was there, during a two-day conference, that I was made aware of the real me.

I had discovered my sinfulness during the preaching of the Jordanian pastor Rev. Zomot. I knew I was not the *bon enfant* I thought I was. God's Spirit had invaded my soul. He had not left any stone unturned—or so I thought. I had surrendered my life to Christ and to doing His will, and had experienced a change unknown to me until then. He healed me inside. My bitterness at life was gone. Moreover, He had baptized me with love for my Muslim family and friends. What else could there be that needed work? I thought He was done with me. But not so!

We were seated around the dinner table at this Baptist village, with probably thirty or forty people. That was quite a crowd for those of us from the church in East Jerusalem. We had not known such numbers, except maybe during revival meetings. Not only had my physical family grown after reuniting with my aunt and her children, but now, just as importantly, my spiritual family had also grown.

What really surprised me at that gathering was the presence of Baptists from a Jewish background. I had heard about them from the missionaries that visited our small church. But this was the first time I had seen them and shared a meal with them—and the honest truth is, I was not ready for this!

All of a sudden I was facing a moment of truth within my own soul. Could I accept these Jews as brothers in the faith? How should I react? Should I simply wear a false smile? That would be hypocritical. But what should I do? Where would I seek counsel, and who was going to give it? I was at a loss.

To make matters worse, one of the men was wearing his Israeli army uniform. *How insensitive*, I thought. *Why rub it in? You do not do this to your brothers in the faith. This is not the place to put on any uniform, especially not the uniform of the victor!* Only one thought lingered in my mind: I wished I had not come.

My mind raced back to the war that had ended. God had spared our lives. But there was even more that I did not discover until the war was over.

During a brief visit to my aunt's house after the war, the same house where I had met Om Ahmad, I learned that two weeks prior to the war, an officer from the Jordanian army had gone there to ask about me. I was wanted. There was need for more draftees. My aunt told them that I had gone to the USA for my education, not knowing that those plans had failed. I was spared. Instead, they took one of my cousins.

I was ecstatic when I heard that news. God had saved me twice, not once—and I had not even been aware of it. I was ecstatic because though I was Arab, yet as a Christian, I could not see myself killing anyone—not even an enemy, a Jew! It had nothing to do with my nationalistic sentiments, but everything to do with my faith. I was happy I did not have to put on a Jordanian army uniform and take part in that war.

The sight of that man wearing his uniform stirred up a number of negative questions and doubts. *How could he claim to be a Christian and take part in a war, any war?* I wondered how many Jordanian soldiers he had killed. This brother had some serious problems, and I set my heart to fix them for him, or possibly fix him.

Against my timid nature, I went to him and introduced myself. He knew I was Arab, of course, just as I knew he was Jewish. He did not need to see me in uniform to identify my ethnic background.

I wanted to force a smile, but I could not. I wanted to ask my question without being accusative. But again I could not. The moment was emotionally charged. So I launched my first missile. "How many Jordanian soldiers did you kill during the war?"

I did not see a need to make any further explanation. My assumptions were clear. My mind was made up. To me, he was already guilty. It was only a matter of making him feel the guilt. He probably passed it by, and as a Christian I thought my responsibility was to bring back his dead conscience to life. I told myself I was doing this partly for him. He needed to wake up to reality. To Christian reality!

With a smile on his face, he said that he had concerns about this himself. He said he prayed to the Lord to spare him that experience. The Lord had answered his prayers. He did not have to do battle. He worked in the kitchen!

He went on to explain to me that drafting in Israel was compulsory, and one cannot excuse oneself out of it, even if he were a Christian. He added that he did not have time to go to his village and change before arriving at the Baptist village, therefore the uniform he was wearing.

His explanations and his answer were revelatory. But more so his general attitude! My accusations did not offend him. He was able to contain my anger with grace. There was a sincere smile on his face as he spoke, and there was humility. He did not come across as one who had just won a war.

I thought the encounter with this Jewish man and the accusations I was firing at him were about his sinfulness, his uniform—about making him feel the guilt! Actually, I was probably using my so-called Christian attitude to sweep away some of the shame I felt about losing the war. My accusations, in fact, revealed my own sinfulness, exposed my biases. My old sinful nature was still lurking on the inside. How sinful can man be? How sinful can a Christian be?

As I think back of that encounter, I am grateful for it—grateful that God did not allow my vengeful and hateful attitudes to live with me any longer! Of all people, God used a Jewish brother in the faith to bring inner healing to my soul. His grace and his graciousness helped melt my arrogance. Bent on shaming him, I was put to shame myself.

I put my hand on his, looked him in the eye and asked for his forgiveness. I was in the wrong, not him. His loving spirit, rather the Spirit of love within him, swept over me. We embraced. He was a brother; a Jewish brother. My mind accepted the facts. My heart was overwhelmed with joy.

Initially, I attended the American College of Jerusalem, a small liberal arts college located in West Jerusalem. I was admitted as a sophomore student. But my dream of pursuing a degree in engineering was not to be fulfilled. I had to content myself with a major in psychology. I also continued working part time at the Baptist bookstore in East Jerusalem.

Wanting to make good on my promise to serve God, I began taking a Bible course on the Book of John offered by my denomination in Haifa. Every Monday afternoon I rode the bus from Jerusalem to Tel Aviv and from there to Haifa, attended the course, stayed the night and traveled back early the next morning in time to make it to class. A year into that, I decided to seek proper seminary training.

The year was 1969. I was twenty-two years old. It had been ten years since I had run away from the orphanage in Bethany, seeking a sense of family, and it had been restored. Those ten years had worked wonders in my life. And yet I know that time alone can never bring healing or restore broken relationships. It was God who worked wonders during those years.

Now it was time to move on. God had been good to me.

I owed Him my life, and I was about to deliver on my promise to serve Him. I left my hometown, Jerusalem, to go to the Arab Baptist Seminary in Lebanon. A whole new chapter was about to begin.

6

Life in Beirut

WHILE the Southern Baptists had established a number of churches in Middle Eastern countries, including Jordan, Israel and Egypt, it was in Lebanon that they set up a seminary. The institution overlooked the city of Beirut with a breathtaking view of the Mediterranean. Back in those years, Lebanon was nicknamed the Switzerland of the East, and rightly so. I arrived in the fall of 1969, one month or so after classes started.

The student body at the seminary was quite small, yet diverse, with students from seven or eight Arab countries. Most were single, ranging in age from late teens to mid-twenties. One or two married couples also attended. The courses in the three-year program were generally easy, devised for the most part for students with a high school diploma. Even so, a number of students who had not finished high school were also part of the program. The faculty, on the other hand, seemed to be well-qualified, and most bent over backwards to accommodate the students.

A beautiful Egyptian girl named Evelyn had answered God's prompting and joined the seminary in Lebanon. Unwed young women were usually denied entry, but they made an exception for Evelyn, and at nineteen she was admitted in the fall of 1968. She was one year ahead of me in her seminary education. Not only was she adorably beautiful, but also extremely intelligent, popular with students and faculty, and always making top grades. Before I knew it we became competitors, each trying to outdo the other. Thankfully, that did not last long; after a few months, that competitive spirit turned into a passionate love story worthy of a novel.

It had been one full year since I had quit the American College of Jerusalem to come to the Baptist Seminary in Beirut. In this metropolis were a number of universities of varying reputation. Yet it was practically impossible to transfer any of my credits from the American College. Israel and all it offered, educationally or otherwise, was blacklisted.

Having committed my life to the service of God and the Arab people, I didn't see the need to further my secular education. I had come to this city to receive an education in biblical interpretation, in the art of preaching and whatever else it took to prepare for a devoted life of Christian ministry. But Evelyn would not hear any of it. With her constant prodding, I found myself pursuing two degrees and three majors at the same time: one degree in theology, and the other in psychology and philosophy.

I was in my first-year at the Arab University of Beirut and finishing my second year at the seminary. I was receiving two kinds of education: one was supposed to help me fulfill my promise to serve God; the other seemed like a plot to destroy every faith foundation I had, apparently designed to deny the very existence of the God I planned to serve. I had set myself on a collision course without initially realizing it.

I lived months on end in mental torment. Was it a mistake to attend the university? Or a mistake to go to seminary? How on earth was I supposed to resolve this? I could have taken the easy way out by dropping my university education altogether. But what would I do later in my ministry if and when such issues showed up? I could not run away every time.

Thankfully, not every philosopher is Albert Camus, Jean Paul Sartre, or Nietzsche. There were philosophers like Immanuel Kant, René Descartes and Jacques Ellul, among others, who expressed belief in God in one way or another. Their works lifted me out of my bottomless pit. Through it all, I grew stronger as a believer, and eventually completed both tracks of my education.

Our days at the Baptist Seminary always started with Bible devotions. Faculty, students, visiting pastors and preachers took turns speaking. A face we got accustomed to was that of Mr. Dunn, a kind man with a very gentle spirit. He headed up the Baptist Center for Radio and Television. His offices and the studios were located in the basement of one of the seminary buildings. We never said much to each other, just nodded in greeting. I knew who he was, and he knew me by name. This one morning he was there seated as usual at the rear of the worship hall. But this time, something unusual happened.

We were beginning to exit the worship hall. I was busy talking to other students. Mr. Dunn was standing outside. His eyes caught mine, and he immediately smiled and winked at me. I wasn't quite sure why. We were heading to class, and I suppose he was heading to his office, but he stopped me halfway. He said he had heard me pray that morning and liked the quality of my voice. Then he asked to see me later, during a break in classes.

In class that morning I was there, but my mind was somewhere else, fixated on my brief exchange with Mr. Dunn. I didn't dare assume too much, despite the obvious connection between what he had said and his work with radio. I didn't want to get my hopes up. But I couldn't help thinking about it.

I still had one more year to go at the seminary. I wouldn't be able to accept a full-time job in Christian radio, if that was what Mr. Dunn wanted to discuss with me. I had no idea what was involved. But then, if he were to offer me a job, I'm sure he had his reasons. I couldn't help looking at my watch every few seconds. It felt like time was standing still.

Finally, the class was over. I was the first one out of the door. I knew where the studios were located, but I'd never been there. I stopped to catch my breath, then gently knocked on the door. Seconds later I found myself seated in the middle of a cluster of bulky machines, with Mr. Dunn's desk at one end. I guessed they must be recording machines, but I had no clue how to work them.

The break between classes was only fifteen minutes; I was going to miss my usual cup of tea. But that didn't matter. Mr. Dunn picked up where he had left off, expressing his confidence that if tested the quality of my voice would prove to be good. Seconds later, he walked me into an adjacent room with a chair, a small table and a microphone. There were no windows other than a small, double-glassed one between the two rooms. It felt dead in there. He made me sit down, then walked out and closed the doors after him. I could see him through that small window, pulling up a chair and facing me between the machines. I could hear his voice asking me to say something, so I said my name, where I was from, and quoted a verse of Scripture.

He stood up, opened the doors to the dead room, and invited me out. "That's all," he said. "I was right. You have a good quality voice." This was the third time he had said that. Except this time, he didn't stop there. He asked if I would be willing to work with him. I asked for a day or two before giving him an answer.

As it was, I did not need even one day to make a decision. By that afternoon I had made up my mind. I didn't ask what I would do, how many hours I would work, or even how much money I was going to make. I desperately needed income, any income. I had been supporting myself working odd jobs at the seminary to pay off my tuition, and ended up each month with some Lebanese liras for pocket money. By the first week of the next month, I was broke. I had to hitchhike to downtown Beirut to go to church, or when push came to shove, to simply walk. Even a part-time job at the Baptist Center assured me of much-needed income.

Evelyn and I had lived a passionate love story, except that a happy ending did not seem to be in sight. Her father was vehemently opposed to her marrying a Palestinian, especially a penniless Palestinian. As I said yes to Mr. Dunn that afternoon, I felt a minute or two closer to the day when I would be able to go to Egypt again and approach Evelyn's parents to ask for her hand in marriage. (My first attempt at that eighteen months earlier ended with a threat from her dad to have me killed. Thankfully, I had tested the waters by phone and not in person.)

I went into Christian radio with absolutely no formal training. There is definitely much more to radio than just voice. Since I was hired uniquely based on my voice, I assumed that I was expected to speak on air; they did not need a good voice to work the equipment. Not that I knew anything of that either. My formal (and up till then, incomplete) education was in psychology, philosophy and theology—not communications or a technical field.

By the time I began earning money, Evelyn had graduated and gone back to Egypt to be with her family. Though I had a year left at the seminary, and two at the university, she did not seem to mind marrying a student. More importantly, she stood firm against her father's threats. We were madly in love. Faced with his daughter's stubborn passion toward this Palestinian student, Evelyn's dad finally gave in. Six months into my job, we wed. It was Christmas of 1971. Evelyn was twenty-two; I was twenty-four.

7

New Skills

GOD had kept His side of the bargain by keeping our family safe during the Six-Day War. I was about to begin to keep my side of it. His part of the bargain did not take long—only one night, the time it took the Israeli Army to take over Jerusalem. My part of the bargain—to serve Him—would take the rest of my life. The bargain I proposed, similar though not identical to Jacob's bargain, may not sound quite equitable: one night versus one life. Yet the fact is that were it not for His keeping us alive that night, we wouldn't have a life to live. I owed it to Him.

My career in Christian radio had just begun. There was a lot for me to learn—in fact, all of it! I had on-the-job training in every aspect of the work: writing radio scripts, pushing the record and play buttons, splicing tape, putting a program together. Mr. Dunn, my teacher and trainer, was essentially an electronics engineer, not a communicator. His help was indispensable with the technical aspects of the job, but the rest he left to me to learn on my own.

In more ways than one, producing radio programs became a question of trial and error, hit and miss. I tried one way and hoped it worked. If not, I tried another, and so on. Ahead of me was another very sharp learning curve.

What I really needed to learn was how to effectively share the gospel. If my past experience could serve as an example, it only served as a bad one. In my first attempt, with my friend Ahmad, the grandson of our landlady in the Jewish quarter of Jerusalem, I failed miserably. I wanted to avoid that, but no one had shown me how.

Our seminary training not only failed to open our eyes to the Muslim majority among whom we lived, but it also failed to train us in how to communicate the gospel in a fashion that would make sense to them. Now I was expected to do that over the radio to untold numbers of people! It was an awesome responsibility given to an apprentice. How unprepared I was!

Combining the new trade I was learning with some of my seminary training—expository preaching and pastoral counseling—and adding to that a few drops of psychology and human understanding, I began to create my own talk programs. I was far from confident; not only were my programs in the test tube, but so was I!

Months into my job, my brother Salem, now a doctor, visited us in Lebanon. Years ago he had been the first to challenge me with the truths of the Bible by offering me a New Testament. He was also the first of my family to hear me speak on the radio, and was not too impressed. Without mincing words, he said, "You do not have to raise your voice when you speak."

Raising my voice was not the only problem I had. Nevertheless, people across the Middle East and North Africa were tuning in and listening. My listeners were kind and forgiving for the most part. There was not much else being presented in Christian broadcasting at the time with which to compare or compete. Some listeners began to write to me. They requested a copy of the New Testament. Others asked questions. Before I knew it I had a huge following, and was deeply involved in their lives. The vast majority were of Muslim background.

Christian radio was an eye-opener: Every day I was invited to think not of a small congregation in a single city, like my church in East Jerusalem; instead I was confronted with millions upon millions of people, from Iraq on the east to Morocco on the west, who were mostly Muslim. Here I was, handed the awesome privilege, the weighty responsibility and the unenviable burden of reaching these potential millions of listeners by way of radio.

To the Baptist mission that owned and operated this communications center, radio was only the starting point. Radio was not their business, but only a means to an end, a steppingstone toward a much nobler goal: that of leading and nurturing individuals and groups of people that would come to believe in Christ and follow Him.

It had been five years since that eventful encounter with the Muslim woman who breast-fed me as an infant. It was four years since I promised God to repay my debt of love to my Muslim family. Here I was years later, working out of another basement, this time in Beirut, Lebanon, down on my knees, working to fulfill my promise and my pledge. The tears of Om Ahmad dripping down my neck that hot summer day in 1966 had never dried. My cheeks were still

bearing the marks of her lips. I was finally repaying her debt
of love.

Growing up as a poor child, I did not have much. I did
not have much to give and therefore could not allow myself
the liberty to take or to borrow. To this day, I find it extremely hard to borrow anything. The same was true in ful-
filling my indebtedness to God and to Om Ahmad. Reaching out to our Muslim friends has never been a duty, not for
me. The Muslims are not my mission field. They are family.
Om Ahmad was Muslim before she took up the responsibility of breast-feeding me. She was Muslim after she breast-
fed me. I cannot change that. I don't want to change that.
Though I never set my eyes on her again, yet I see her mir-
rored in every Muslim I meet.

I don't talk with a Muslim to change him. I cannot change
him, even if I wanted to. What would I change him to? A
Christian? I was a "Christian," and I was as sinful as could
be. Will I therefore want to have him changed from a sinful
Muslim to a sinful Christian?

As a Christian, even as a nominal Christian, I knew the
doctrines of Christianity. As a Catholic I believed in every
Christian doctrine there is. I believed in the Trinity. I believed that Christ died for our sins. I believed in heaven and
hell, and scores of other doctrines. But what did that do for
me? Even as the reading of the Bible enlightened me, even as
it corrected some of my thinking, yet I remained at heart the
same person, sinful through and through.

It is true that I was filled with religion. With the true
Christian religion! But so what? It is not my religiosity, nor
my doctrines, nor my Christian birth—if such a thing ex-
ists—that I want to pass on to others. I had a need, and

Christ met that need. My adoptive Muslim family also has needs like I did and do. Christ can meet their needs in the same way He met mine. This is nothing about Christianity. This is everything about Christ.

Twelve short months into my job, I came face to face with a task that was not covered in my practical radio training nor in my job description. A good number of listeners, especially in North Africa, asked me to visit. We had been corresponding for some weeks or even months. Strong relationships were being formed. It was time to have a personal encounter.

Morocco lies at the extreme western end of the Mediterranean Sea. My travels had been limited thus far to my hometown, Jerusalem; my wife's native country, Egypt; and our host country where we resided and made a living, Lebanon. I had some general familiarity with the Middle East. Morocco was part of the unknown, in more ways than one.

It was the summer of 1972. I had done my best, which was not always good by any standard, to communicate the love of God to anyone willing to listen. I had spent twelve short months on the job. I had set sail without a compass, without really knowing where I was heading. I had the voice. The job was varied and exciting. Little did I realize at the time that I was starting on a long spiritual journey. Only five short years before, I had set my heart to repay two debts of love. At the time, I had no idea whatsoever how I was going to fulfill my vow. But God did. I only said yes. He arranged all the details.

8

Notes and Anecdotes

JULY of 1972 was upon us. Weeks of preparations had preceded that date. I had contacted every listener who had expressed a sincere desire to know more about Christ or the Christian faith. I had written back to every one, and as the months and weeks passed, we were convinced we needed to go a step beyond our correspondence. We needed to spend time face to face with those who desired to see us.

Missionary journeys were only things we had read about in the book of Acts. But now, my wife and I were on our first missionary journey. We were heading to Morocco.

It was very much a step into the unknown. We were Middle Easterners. They were North Africans. Our cultures, our languages and our religious backgrounds were different.

We had about seventy individuals we hoped to see in four weeks, and we needed to see them individually. We could not bring them together. Their questions, their needs were quite similar, as was the general environment in which they were born and raised. Yet we were their sole and only contact; we could be trusted specifically because we did not live in their country. They could not share their secret aspirations with their own countrymen for obvious reasons. Four weeks, seventy contacts, fifteen different locations throughout Morocco—it was a huge undertaking.

The trip was long, in more than a geographical sense. It stretched our understanding and often exposed our limitations. We found ourselves spending precious time debating points of Christian doctrine they had a hard time understanding, let alone accepting.

The Trinity was exceptionally a hot issue. Allah, which is God's name to all the Arabs, Christians and Muslims alike, could not have a Son! Human experience interpreted such terminology in only one way, the same way that humans bear and birth sons. Their understandable attitude: God forbid that He be involved in such behavior!

We had learned through the letters received over the previous twelve months what the basic questions were. But we did not necessarily have the answers. Having been born in traditional Christian homes ourselves, we had accepted the Christian doctrines by faith. We were not quite able to understand the answers ourselves, let alone explain them. How can God be One in Three and Three in One?

We also had to deal with security issues. In our own minds we perceived ourselves as guests. Our listeners had invited us to come—we did not go knocking on their doors. They chose to listen to the radio broadcasts. They chose to write. They chose to invite us to come and see them. But that, as we were to learn, was all beside the point.

I remember, for example, the trip we made to see Hameed, who lived outside the city. He could not be reached by public transportation, unless you include donkeys. As it turned out, our trip did include a donkey ride. It also included walking the last several hundred yards on foot after the owner of the donkey asked us to get off, took his fare and went his way.

There was only one small house in sight. Everything else was desert. We made our way to it, knocked on the door and waited. A man came to the door and let us in.

Given the rudimentary setting of his home, only a sincere and serious seeker would try to establish contact with the outside world from such a place. Writing back to him from Lebanon was not a problem for us. We only had to drop that letter in the mailbox next door. But for him, it was very different.

Listening to Christian radio was also a challenge. His wife was still a devout Muslim. He could not tell her he was interested in the Christian faith, or that he was corresponding with a Christian center in Lebanon, or that he was reading the Bible. To this day, I do not know what he said to her to justify our visit to their house. We had sent him a Bible at his request, which he received. As soon as his wife left the room, he fetched it from under the mattress.

Our two-hour visit was quite disconcerting. Every time his wife came into the room, we had to change the subject. Every time she left, we were back answering his questions about Christ and the Christian faith. The time had not come for him to share his newfound faith with her or with anyone else. We were not about to ruin that.

As we stood to leave, he would not let us go. As guests, we were expected to give our hosts three full days. That was the custom with friends and family. As friends you are expected to share your life, your time with them. Those were the host's days. But then there were the guest's days on top of that—you were expected to spend three additional days as a guest, to show that you valued this relationship as much as the host did. Six days in all, at minimum!

But because we were not from the culture and had a tight schedule, we managed to leave after a couple of hours. That did not sit well with our host. We were offending him. We also had not eaten, which doubled the offense. Despite it all, he graciously asked his wife to prepare a gift for us—three live chickens, one for each day we were expected to stay in his home!

That was a very humbling experience. For him, listening to Christian radio and reading his Bible was a major challenge. Then he had to write letters and travel to town to mail them, and to receive our mail! Our trip from Lebanon to his home was more like a vacation than what he faced day in and day out. We had come to encourage him and teach him in the ways of the Lord, and we ended up being students ourselves. That was one of many lessons God had in store for us.

The most amazing part, however, was knowing that we had a brother there in the middle of nowhere. He had a different culture, a different religious background, a different skin color, but he was our brother—a Kingdom brother, where borders, nationality, color and, above all, religious background mean absolutely nothing. We had not turned him from a "Muslim" into a "Christian," inasmuch as we did not change his nationality. He remained who he was, a married Moroccan dark-skinned Muslim male who loved and followed Christ. We did not speak negatively about his traditional faith,

Islam. We never do. Our brother had a need, and Christ met it. It was his personal decision to love and follow Him.

Over the four weeks that we spent in Morocco, we met many other brothers and sisters. In each and every case, Christ was real, very real, probably more real to them than we at times are willing to admit. He had appeared to some in dreams. He had healed others. In one case a young man experienced firsthand the difference that praying to Jesus Christ can bring about. He was not yet His follower, but he had seen His power, and he longed to know Him.

Our trip was coming to a close. We had been blessed beyond measure. We had seen the work of Christ in ways that we did not expect. We went to minister, but we were ministered to. Four weeks before, the undertaking seemed so huge and impossible. These brothers and sisters did not know each other. They did not trust each other. They did not want to bring shame to their families by being accused of forsaking their faith. They also had well-founded security concerns, more so than we did for ourselves.

But now, four short weeks into it, certain things were beginning to change—things not related to their circumstances, but to their perspective. Either our zeal, our ignorance, or both led us to invite about twenty of our listeners on a two-day retreat. That would be their first chance to know that there were other listeners besides them. It also meant that their interest in the Christian faith would become public knowledge. This was a risky undertaking, but we decided to go for it—or more correctly, *they* decided to go for it. We both knew that they would have to live with the consequences, but we suggested it and they agreed.

We came, we worshiped, we sang. We studied the Bible

and we broke bread together. At the end of those two days, some of them followed the Lord's ordinance and were baptized. A church was being born. A church made up of Muslim brothers and sisters. These were followers of Christ, but they were not "Christians." I was beginning to repay Om Ahmad the debt of love!

9

Plagued with
Too Much History

Upon our return to Lebanon, my wife and I could not contain our joy. We had never seen so many people become followers of Christ in so short a time. It was true that these brothers and sisters were just beginning their journey of knowing Christ, following Him and imitating His life. But they had made the decision. Their water baptism, to which many of us attach no special significance, was their sign and seal. We had to tell everyone what we had seen and heard.

One of the people dearest to me was my father, whose blessing and approval I had long sought. I had left Jerusalem three years before to go to Lebanon. By the end of 1972 I had graduated from seminary and married my Egyptian bride. My father had not come to my graduation or wedding, and had never met Evelyn. I wanted his blessing on my marriage and his approval of my ministry. I did not really know if he believed in what I had dedicated my life to do. It was time to find out.

A trip to Jerusalem to meet my father would be a new experience for Evelyn. As an Egyptian, she had never set foot in Israel. (Years later, after President Anwar Sadat of Egypt made his historical trip to Israel, my wife would say that she made that trip before he did!)

The trip would also be a major undertaking. Though Israel is situated immediately to the south of Lebanon, we could not drive or fly south. From Lebanon, we had to go to Syria, to Jordan, and then to Israel. There were three border crossings with two separate sets of forms to fill out at each, and a different set of questions to answer each time.

Once in Jordan, we stayed a couple of days to rest. We needed every ounce of strength for the road trip from Amman to Jerusalem. Though only a short forty miles that normally could be traveled in sixty minutes, it took eight long hours. At the end of the fourth day, we were happy to be home in Jerusalem.

Grooms in the Middle East take pride in the beauty of their brides. I wanted everyone in my family to meet Evelyn, to admire her beauty and commend me for having made such a good choice. But above everything else, I wanted my father to accept her. I had every reason to expect him to respect my choice of a wife; having been the victim of an arranged marriage, my father had learned his lesson well. Still, I sought his acceptance.

My wife had her own concerns. She came from a different culture and spoke a different dialect. She was young and was married to the youngest son in the family. She knew that as the youngest son, I had limited influence on my old father. But she had the right attitude. She came with a sincere desire to make my family her own.

Evelyn and I were still bubbling over from our experience in Morocco the month before, so when the first chance presented itself, we began sharing about the trip. The testimonies were still very fresh and colorful. My father and stepmother were Christians, and they seemed happy to hear what we were telling them. But there was one small detail about which they both felt uneasy, especially my father: the names!

The names of the Moroccan men and women whose testimonies we were recounting were obviously Muslim: Ahmad, Mohammed, Ali and Fatima. "Muslims could not possibly become followers of Christ," my dad declared adamantly. There was no changing his mind.

During the wars of Napoleon, the Swiss had this saying: "Les peuples heureux n'ont pas d'histoire." Translated literally, it means that happy peoples have no history.

As it is, the Middle East is nothing but history, with Jerusalem at center stage. There, people have been blessed—or plagued—with too much history. My father was only repeating what he had heard and learned from his forefathers. History again! To him, and to innumerable millions before and after him, names have meaning. They also have connotations and implications. Many if not most were loaded with religious overtones and undertones.

My dad was given the name *Shehadeh* (Arabic for begging) because his mother begged God for him. She had three girls before he was born, and she longed to have a boy. He remained an only son.

The name *Hanna* (Arabic for John) that I was given at birth meant that I was Christian, even before I knew it myself. The name was tagged with a religion. In that sense, my religion was decided for me, just like my name. As a matter of fact, the name was born of my religion, and was chosen on its basis.

I was trapped in that cage of names as much as my father was until my trip to Morocco. That is exactly how I had seen my friend Ahmad years before. I had seen him through his religious identity, and the key to it was his name. His first name, his father's name, as well as his family name! Names, names, and more names!

In a moment of sheer foolishness, I wished I could take every Middle Eastern name and change it to something else. Even if my wish were to come true, our people would find some other way to bring to the surface the differences that divide us. (Not that this is not done already: Many countries in that region write one's religion on one's passport or ID card.) But if I could change people's names, I might at least delay the process of identification by religion, with the mental images, sectarian divisions and shameful prejudices that follow.

The Middle East religious landscape has underlined these identifications in crimson red—red as in blood! A lot of harm has been brought on people simply for the name they carry. The tragedy is that they did not choose those names themselves.

Most people in the Middle East, and other places, identify the name *Moshe* as being Jewish. But this is not an unusual name at all. Many Arabs, both Christian and Muslim, give the name *Moussa* to their sons—the *same name*, just spelled and pronounced a bit differently. The spelling and pronunciation are enough to identify the ethnic background, and often the religion, of the person. What may follow in discrimination and other forms of harassment can be too shameful to describe!

It is a shame because it is neither fair nor right to have to live with such consequences just for being given one name over another. It is not fair because a name can be utterly meaningless—completely void of cultural or religious content—to the one who carries it. But to the hearer, it is loaded. Moshe is not necessarily Jewish, despite his name. Hanna is not necessarily Christian, also despite his name. And the same applies to Mohammed, who may not necessarily be Muslim! How do we begin changing all that?

What if we allowed ourselves to imagine, just imagine, making Hanna Muslim, Moshe Christian and Mohammed Jewish? Impossible, you say? I wonder why? It seems we have allowed ourselves to become hostage to our names, and beyond that, to our religions! Is that how it was meant to be?

Despite his age, or possibly because of it, my dad was glued to his perspective, and the testimonies from our Moroccan visit made no difference. I wished he had come with us; many times seeing is believing. But the trip was behind us, and no amount of convincing could change his mind.

On second thought, Dad's conviction that Muslims could not become followers of Christ was only his surface problem. His real problem was unbelief. To him, Christ was simply unable to make followers from among Muslims. My dad was limiting the power of Christ. Maybe what he needed was not more testimonies, but more of Christ!

Aside from our disagreement over whether Muslims could become followers of Christ, our time with my family was well spent. My wife was well received. She brought gifts for everyone, and they bought gifts for her. That was a good sign.

Our visit to the old city was very memorable for her. I showed her my old school, right next to the New Gate. She worshiped with the Jerusalem Baptist church. Their number had not changed much; they had moved by then from a basement to an old house in another part of town.

I took her to the Christian and Jewish quarters in town. We walked the *Via Dolorosa*. But it was far different from showing tourists around for tips, like I did when I was in my teens. This was my wife, and I was taking pride in our city.

I showed her the room where seven of us lived at one point. I was not ashamed to let her see my humble history. If she had any qualms about who I was, they were gone now. One spot we missed for lack of time was Bethany, the Catholic orphanage where I spent my childhood.

I also took her to Rafeedia, where I had my encounter with Om Ahmad, my nursing Muslim mother. Here were my roots. We spent a couple of days at my sister's house, before returning to Jerusalem. It was now time to head back to Lebanon. We dreaded the long and tedious journey ahead of us, but there was no way out of it. Lebanon had become our home, and Christian radio was now my mission.

My wife and I lived a total of seven years in Lebanon. In Beirut we were blessed with a first son. We gave him the name *Bassem* (smiling). It is an ethnically Arab name, not Christian or Muslim. We wanted to save him some of the hassles we had with our "Christian" names.

In the Middle East people are not given middle names. A person is identified only by his first name and family name. In that sense our son was safer—neither his first name nor our family name, *Shahin* (Arabic for falcon), betrayed him as a Christian!

I ended up being married to both my wife and my job. I enjoyed tremendously what I was doing. I was meeting a lot of people, both in person and through letters. When I got tired of that, I could always hide behind machines and produce programs. My presentation on radio was mellowing. I was full of myself when I started. By the third or fourth year, that began to change.

But things were not going well in my marriage. I had fought for my wife, and she had fought for me. After a romantic courtship that lasted two years, we were finally married. Two years into it, however, our relationship was souring. I was giving much more attention to mass communication than communication with my wife. However, thanks to good counseling from our pastor, we were soon back on track.

10

On the Move

BY THE SPRING of 1975, the political situation had hopelessly deteriorated between the Lebanese government and the Palestinians, which was followed by conflict largely between Christian and Muslim militias. Lebanon was home to large Palestinian communities, many of whom lived in refugee camps. Some had been there for decades; they had fled their villages and towns in 1948, during the Israeli-Arab war. Others had come after the 1967 Six-Day War, and still others fled Jordan after the PLO was routed from that country in September of 1970.

First, it was skirmishes; then attacks and mass murders; soon it became a full-blown war, involving virtually all members of society. Everyone seemed to have a stake in it, including other regional powers. My small family and I were guests, with no political or other interests whatsoever. I was there on a mission, but after a few months of living the harsh conditions of that war, it became impossible for me to pursue my ministry. The road to work was very dangerous. Any day could have been my last.

In our predicament we had nothing to win and every-thing to lose. Lebanese militias were dynamiting every Palestinian they could get their hands on, or so the rumors went. The Palestinians were returning the favor. I could speak the Lebanese dialect, but I was born Palestinian. Ethnicity, religious affiliations, names and even dialects were all becoming liabilities. Each of these elements sharpened the divide in a once peaceful country.

While everyone spoke Arabic, differing ethnic groups had their own dialect. Though differences were subtle, a single word could often identify a speaker. The Lebanese word for tomato is *banadoora*. The Palestinian rendition is *bandora*. Close, but not quite the same. It became well known that people were losing their lives if they were stopped at the wrong checkpoint—all due to their pronunciation of the word tomato!

This is when we decided to leave. I did not want to lose my life because of my dialect, my ethnicity, my name, my religion or any other sectarian reason.

Gunshots, mortar and all sorts of live ammunition were clear and loud during the day, and more so during the night hours. Over the last few weeks we had been sleeping in the hallway in the interior of our apartment, but it still did not keep the noise out. Our three-year-old son, Bassem, began to have frequent nightmares. I was quite attached to my mission, but by the latter part of 1975, the situation had become unbearable, and I realized we had to move. There was only one problem to resolve: Where would we go?

Jerusalem was not a possibility; I had lost my residence. Though I could have gone to Jordan, I was not really familiar with that country. (East Jerusalem and the West Bank were under Jordanian jurisdiction at the time I was born, so I carried a Jordanian passport and was considered Jordanian.)

In the midst of our confusion and distress, a letter unexpectedly arrived in the mail. We were surprised by the US postmark, but even more by the sheer fact that something, anything at all, had arrived in the mail. The war had disrupted every aspect of life in Lebanon. The timing of the letter also seemed to be divinely appointed, bringing a glimmer of hope into our hopeless situation.

It was from one of my former colleagues at the seminary, now in the USA, who told me of an opening in his organization; he felt we would be good candidates. In the meantime he suggested we go to Egypt and wait until our paperwork was processed and our visas issued.

His proposal made a great deal of sense. My in-laws lived in Egypt at the time, and they welcomed us with open arms, despite the size of our family and the limited space they had. (There were three of us now, with a second child on the way.)

Our days in Egypt extended into weeks, then into months. I spent much of those long days reading; there was not much else I could do. It was obvious I had not learned my lesson well. Years before I waited in vain for my student visa to the USA. Ten years later, I was in limbo again—waiting for paperwork and visas to the USA. Except this time I had a wife and a son to provide for, and no bookstore where I could earn some money. We left Lebanon with a few thousand dollars, and since we didn't have to pay any rent, that money was good for quite some time. But there was no means in sight of generating any income.

By the end of the second month, I received an invitation

from a local congregation to preach. I was not ready for that. Not that I had not preached before, but I just never saw myself as a preacher. I could hide behind a microphone and say a few words on a Christian radio program, but preparing long-winded messages and delivering them to a crowd was just not one of my strengths.

On the other hand, I did not want my in-laws to lose face in their town and among their people. This was not a matter of right or wrong, but of bringing honor, not shame, to my family. Much of the social fabric and behavior in Middle Eastern communities is based on this system. I was a seminary graduate and by definition, therefore, a preacher. Pressure was building on me to accept the invitation.

But I couldn't preach. I had studied the Bible, both personally and at the seminary. I had studied Bible commentaries. I could read both Hebrew and Greek. All of that did not make me a preacher. To me the Bible was a sealed book. I enjoyed reading it and learning something from it for my own life and edification. Turning the little I gleaned from it into a meaningful sermon that could fit it into the everyday living of an audience was a different ballgame. I could not bring it to life for my hearers.

I was given two weeks' notice, and time was running out. I was at my wit's end. There was only one resort I hadn't properly tapped: *prayer!*

I began to focus on prayer and further readings of the Scriptures. By the middle of the second week of my extended prayer times, the words I read started to make sense. Suddenly the dots were being connected for me. I did not connect them. I didn't concoct anything. What happened was not of my personal making. It was as if, suddenly and without prior warning, the Scriptures were opened before my eyes. I continued to spend seven or eight hours a day on my knees with nothing but the Bible.

The date was now upon me. The church's invitation was for a week of revival meetings, something I had attended but never personally conducted. It was an awesome responsibility. The Lord's grace was sufficient to carry me through.

About four months into our refugee status and two months into my preaching, our second son, *Shadi* (Arabic for singing), was born. Not that our lives necessarily corresponded to the name we gave him. We were still in limbo waiting for the US paperwork to come through. To add to our challenges, the authorities were only renewing my visa two weeks at a time, and that meant making the trip from the town where my in-laws lived to downtown Cairo every two weeks to ask for a renewal. It was clear that we needed to leave Egypt and seek another country.

At the close of thirteen weeks of daily preaching at this church, the leaders came to the home of my in-laws to thank us and see us off. They came with a monetary gift: fifty Egyptian pounds (the equivalent of about seventy five dollars at the time). That was all they could afford.

I was not expecting any money; it was an honor and blessing simply to have a ministry. Besides, I still had some savings left, so I didn't really need the money. And more importantly, it seemed to me that the church could put these funds to much better use. The church building was virtually a skeleton—unfinished brick walls and a dirt floor. The pews, the platform, the pulpit—everything spoke of need. I could not possibly accept their gift!

I thought I was doing the church a favor by not accepting

their gift, as well as conveying the message that my ministry was unto God. Why should men pay me back, especially if I can support myself? God may have taught me how to preach, but I still need to gain an insight into how people think.

To them, I came across as prideful. I was looking down on their gift. So they turned to my mother-in-law and complained. After their visit, she summoned me into her room and said, "Hanna, learn to *ride the donkey*." (By this she was alluding to Jesus, who humbled Himself by riding a donkey into Jerusalem.)

I did some soul-searching. In my teens I had worked to earn my money. I had worked my way through seminary and university without any financial help from my family. (My family was not in a position to help anyway!) I had never learned to receive from others. In the end I had to swallow my pride and take their gift. They were right, I was wrong.

The time had come for our young family of four to leave Egypt. We were on the road again—this time with more responsibility and less money! Above all, I had no job, and four mouths to feed. We flew from Cairo to Amman, Jordan. That was our only possible destination. My Jordanian passport served me well.

I had visited Jordan before, and traveled through it on my way from Jerusalem to Lebanon a couple of times. I had family living there back then, but no longer. Outside one Baptist pastor, I had no church connections. Jordan offered our family few possibilities.

Once at Amman airport, we got into a cab and asked to be taken to a downtown hotel. The "hotel" we were dropped off at was more like a dingy, stinky apartment building that was definitely not designed for families. There was no privacy; the restrooms were out in the hallway. Bugs were everywhere.

I knew we had to leave that place. But where would we go? Over half a million Lebanese refugees had flooded into Jordan, causing a severe housing shortage and skyrocketing rents. Like us, they had left their homes because of the war. I had lost my job, and my family had no decent place to live. We were really stuck!

By the second week at that wretchedly miserable hotel, we had had it. The weather was pleasant, so we spent as much time outdoors as we possibly could. During one such outing, we ran into an old acquaintance from Lebanon. Though Amman was not a very big city, still we found it intriguing to meet someone we knew, but we did not think much of it at the time. He was just another casualty of the war.

The next morning there was a knock on our door. That was one other "blessing" of this hotel—no "do not disturb" sign to hang on the door knob. Its absence seemed to imply that we could be disturbed by almost anyone at any time. I had complained to the management, but nothing was done.

What we didn't know was that it would be the last time we would be disturbed like that. At the door was our acquaintance from Lebanon. He told us to pack and get ready to leave. We were moving out.

It didn't take us long to get ready. We were soon checking out of the hotel. To our utter amazement, our hotel bill was paid. Beyond a shadow of doubt, we could see that God's finger was in this.

Soon all four of us—my wife, our two sons and myself—were settled in a one-room apartment. It was not one bedroom, but one *room*—a living room, dining room and bedroom all in one. This was nothing strange to me. Back in Jerusalem, as many as seven of us lived together in one room. And just as it was in Jerusalem, the kitchen and restroom were outside, right around the corner. I only hoped that if we ever grew to a family of seven, we would find a larger apartment!

It was obvious that we had not been showered with material blessings. After all, what God had provided was shelter: a room, not a house! That became our home, and it was enough to give us confidence that He would take care of us.

I had turned down an invitation to be the pastor of a church in Jordan soon after my graduation from seminary years before. I was very content being involved in Christian radio, and I was not a preacher. Now things had changed. Having been empowered to preach during our time in Egypt, I was more confident that I could serve as a pastor. I did not have the luxury of doing what I liked, anyway.

Instead of seeking employment, however, we just waited, not even knowing how to pursue a pastoral opening. I guess I was hoping a church would somehow hear about me and ask me to become their pastor. It was not long, though, before I came to find out that every church in the country had more than its share of pastors. Any vacancies that existed before the Lebanese civil war had been filled by refugee Lebanese pastors. Our five-month stint in Egypt put us at the end of the line for housing and employment. Still, I would not have traded our stay in Egypt for anything. God had touched me there. He had opened my eyes and my heart to His Word.

And, as it turned out, we did not have to wait long in Jordan, after all.

11

A New Beginning

B Y THE MIDDLE of our second week in Jordan, an offer for employment arrived literally at our door. The manager of the British Airways sales office in Amman came to our apartment and said he heard that I had mastered a few languages. He decided I could be useful in the airline business. The job offer he placed in my lap was as unexpected as the one I received less than five years earlier, when the manager of the Baptist Center for Radio and Television heard me pray and decided I had a good radio voice.

Making reservations and selling tickets did not require any special gifting, so it did not take me long to learn the trade and excel at it. The manager was a strong Christian and the son of a local pastor. Because of that, many believers bought their tickets at our office. I could not have found a faster way to get to know the evangelical Christian community in our newly adopted country of Jordan.

Within the first weeks of living in Jordan, my wife and I were commissioned by church leadership to start an outreach ministry in a rural area west of Amman. We were also encouraged to move to that part of the countryside. I continued spending my weekdays working for British Airways, for which I was getting increasingly well paid. I spent my free afternoons, weekends and any other time available playing soccer with every willing young man in the neighborhood. One minute I was dressed in my dark blue suit, and the next I was in shorts trying to keep pace with a dozen teenage boys. My wife, meanwhile, socialized with the boys' mothers and sisters.

Our aim was not to present Christianity, not even to present Christ. We lived among them, ate with them and played with them with the sole purpose of living Christ before them. Before we knew it, we had a following. Within three short years we had a congregation of about thirty committed followers of Christ, made up mostly of young people. To us, discipleship was not a course we gave to those young men and women. It was living the life of Jesus before them and with them. Our outreach ministry in the small town of Fheis, Jordan, reflected that informal understanding. Thankfully, no one had taught us otherwise.

Jordan is not a big country. Its roads are well-paved, thus making travel between its cities and towns fairly easy. It was not much of a sacrifice to accept invitations to preach at different evangelical churches. One such church was about forty miles or so to the northwest of where we lived, in Ajloun.

The day was Sunday; I had finished preaching at the only Baptist church in that town and was headed back home to Amman. It was quite common to find soldiers standing on the side of the road with their arms stretched out asking for a ride. Oftentimes there would be two or three standing together. I never stopped for more than one person standing alone. I found it hard to carry out a meaningful discussion with more than one at a time.

I did pass several groups of soldiers that afternoon. A little further down the road, there was one soldier standing alone. I stopped my vehicle. Without hesitation he jumped in and sat next to me in the front seat. He was young, about my age or a little younger. I looked at the badge he had pinned on his chest: Against a dark background, the name Mustapha popped up in bold white letters.

My radio experience was behind me, but what followed sounded much like a radio interview. I asked him where he was going, whether he was married, how many years he had served in the army and some other questions. The first five to ten minutes served as a bridge of trust building. Since I asked him where he was going, I estimated how long I would have him with me. Judging by that, I knew I had a dedicated audience for the next hour or so. I could afford using those first few minutes to get acquainted.

His turn came to ask questions. Although he did not ask about my name, he asked about everything else. He could tell by my accent that I did not quite belong to that part of Jordan. He wondered what I was doing in that region.

For the next few minutes I spoke and he listened. I told him my name and where I was from, which explained my differing accent. I told him that I had been invited to speak at a church in that region. I even gave him a brief outline of the message I had preached that morning. I paused for a few seconds allowing the little I said to sink in. I wanted to get a general reading of his reaction and interest, or possibly the lack of it. Mustapha *was* interested—very interested. His questions kept coming. He wondered what led me to become a preacher.

I spoke about my religious upbringing and the false security that gave me. I did not hide behind my sinful past, nor did I blow it up for him. I said it as it was. I finally explained to him that neither the church nor my religion could pull away my mask of religiosity. In fact, they provided the mask for me. I went on to speak of that eventful experience I had during the revival meetings that his Jordanian compatriot Rev. Zomot preached at the Jerusalem Baptist Church twelve years before. Christ had transformed my life. There was no reason to be ashamed of Him.

I had spoken for about ten minutes. This was not a message I was preaching at some church. This was a friendly interaction. Or at least, I hoped it would be. I paused again. I needed to hear Mustapha. Most of what I shared was completely new to him. His religious background and tradition as a Muslim presented huge doctrinal obstacles. And while I was not discussing doctrines or religions with him, his mind may easily wander into such territory. That would be a minefield. Doctrinal differences between the two faiths are irreconcilable.

A couple of minutes passed in complete silence. We had been together for over forty-five minutes. It wouldn't be long before he would ask to get off and go his way. "What was it that you prayed that evening?" he asked suddenly, referring to that eventful revival service back in Jerusalem. I knew I couldn't honestly remember the exact words my heart uttered. And even if I could, those words were not some magic that were guaranteed to bring about transformation every time someone prayed them. I was driving. I couldn't possibly close my eyes. Plus, Muslims traditionally evoke God with their eyes open. Mustapha shouldn't be offended if I lifted up a short prayer with my eyes on the road. He had asked to know what I prayed. Rather than explain it, I offered to pray the prayer out loud—and I did, right then and there.

A minute or two passed without a word. One more time Mustapha interrupted the silence. He asked to get off. I slowed down, took to the right of the road and stopped. I did not quite know what to expect. I hoped that my act of service would help cover any misgivings I may have created by presenting Christ to him. I had avoided any reference to religions or doctrines. Such a discussion was irrelevant, immaterial. I was a sinner whose life was transformed by Christ. He was just the same, also a sinner. Christ was just as able to transform his life like He did mine.

I knew I was not the Good Samaritan having given him the ride. It was not like I had showed mercy on him, or showered him with my goodness. On the contrary! He was Muslim, and I may have offended him terribly by doing what I did.

On the other hand, there was no guarantee I would see him again, and I wanted to leave something with him just in case he was sympathetic to what I had said. I had several copies of the New Testament in the glove compartment. I reached out, took one, and asked him if he cared to take it. I explained that this book presented more truths about the life-changing Christ than I had time to share with him. Mustapha was now standing outside the car with the door open. He stretched his hand to shake mine, thanked me for the ride, took the New Testament and said, "Brother Hanna, I will see you in heaven."

Glued to my seat, I saw him walk away. I was still parked on the side of the road. My eyes welled up. I could not control my feelings. I had never seen anything like that before. He called me his brother. Mustapha and Hanna—brothers! This cannot be the work of humans. I knew I did not do it. I could not possibly have done it. He did not do it either. Something, somebody was at work here. Without further hesitation, and oblivious to the traffic that was coming on my left side I opened my door, jumped out, ran after him and hugged him.

As I drove off, I laughed and cried. I had one more brother—Mustapha! He did not know anything about my Muslim nursing mother; that is not why he called me brother. He did so because Christ had made us both part of his family. Only Christ works across national, ethnic, cultural and religious divides. To Him, these are futile human inventions that have only caused problems within the human race. To Him, there is no Jew, Christian or Muslim. There is no Arab or Israeli. There is no black or white. We all lose our differences in Him.

I have never forgotten my brother Mustapha. I have no idea of his whereabouts, whether he is still in the army, or if he is still alive! But one thing I know: Christ had done a miracle in His life. Mustapha had joined me in that prayer, confessing his sins and receiving the forgiveness that only Christ can give and the promise of eternal life that comes with it. Mustapha had become a follower of Christ. But he was not a "Christian"! He was a Muslim, with a Muslim name. But he was a follower of Jesus, nonetheless.

The testimony of Mustapha brings back joyful memories. My one concern, though, is what became of him. Has he followed through? Did he take the time to read and study the Arabic New Testament I gave him? Did others see a difference in him? Many other questions come to my mind as I think about him.

I have already stated that it is not my intention to change anyone from one religion to another. I know that religions are different in many aspects. I also know that they are similar in many aspects. Religions are systems: ethical, and sometimes moral, regulatory systems of right and wrong. Religions are systems of approaching deity, and sometimes of defining and regulating human relationships. In this way, any religion is as good as another.

I will not push one religion over another, not even Christianity over Judaism or Islam. I have serious doubts that Christianity can do more for someone than another religion can. Was it not under the banner of Christianity that Hitler committed the ugliest crimes in the history of mankind? No one can turn a blind eye or a deaf ear to historical truths! Religions have caused many wars in the history of mankind, and under its guise much blood was shed.

Yet regretfully, this is not the way most people see and understand religions. Their religions become the answer to everything. Their religions become so sacred in their eyes, they are willing to die and kill defending them. My heart goes out to Mustapha, especially if he followed through with his faith in Christ. By sharing my testimony with him, and indirectly inviting him to allow Christ to invade his life, I may have unintentionally brought physical harm on him. I rejoice in the forgiveness of sins he has received. I also hurt, since doing this may have exposed him to pain and suffering.

My experience with Mustapha, and with scores of others

after that, has often haunted me. Here I was, seeking to re-pay my debt to my Muslim nursing mother, and choosing to do so by directly, and indirectly, inviting my Muslim broth-ers and friends to allow Christ to invade their lives. All this time I have asked myself if I could have repaid my debt of love in a better way, at least without potentially causing any additional hardship! But then, I was only doing what my heart led me to do. I did that uniquely out of love. I did and do that because I want them also to experience the power of Christ to meet their every need, in the same way He met and continues to meet mine.

12

Time for Change

WE DIDN'T plan to have our sons born in different countries—Bassem in Beirut, Lebanon, and Shadi, in Cairo, Egypt. Now that we were in Jordan, a third son was born to us, *Salam* (Arabic for peace). Three years later, our fourth son, *Wadie* (Arabic for meek), would also be born in Jordan. In the Middle Eastern culture, my wife was considered a truly blessed woman for extending the family name and lineage by bringing four males into the world. She actually wanted a baby girl (probably to keep her company in her later years), to the point that she dressed our youngest in pink through his third month!

I also didn't have any plans when I was hired to work for British Airways—I didn't think I would stay there forever, but neither did I expect to move on any time soon. I took each day as it came. The job was exciting and the pay was good. My family and I could fly almost anywhere for little or no money, and we did. We went to London many times to shop, and also took trips to several other countries, including the USA.

By the middle of the third year, with a course or two offered by the company in England, I learned quite a bit. It was not long before other airline companies offered me jobs in Jordan and overseas for much more than what I was earning. It was becoming quite tempting.

However, I was getting pressure from other corners as well. My wife, for one, often reminded me that God had not called me to work for an airline and make a lot of money. I was hearing the same message from preachers, evangelists and other Christian friends who bought their tickets at our office. One of those was an old-time friend from Beirut. Like half a million others, he and his wife also fled the war and moved temporarily to Jordan, and, as is customary in the Middle East, we invited them to stay in our home. During their two weeks with us, my friend did not pass an occasion without impressing on me the need to quit my work and join their ranks. He and his wife worked with Campus Crusade for Christ.

No sooner had they left than other Campus Crusade staffers were introduced to us, and the pressure continued to mount. Toward the end of my third year as a travel agent, the Jordanian national director of Campus Crusade arranged for me to have dinner with Dr. Bill Bright, founder and president of the organization.

It was an unforgettable meeting. There was something unique and compelling about Dr. Bright; it may have been his walk with God, or his prayer life. All through the meal I strongly sensed I was in the presence of a very godly man, and I could not turn a deaf ear to his invitation to join the organization, as I had with his staff.

Until that dinner I doubted the need to quit my job. I

was giving God all my free time. I was pastor of a church, on a volunteer basis. Joining Campus Crusade meant facing the prospect of having to beg others for my personal support. Who wants to be on the receiving end after being on the giving end? To use the words of my mother-in-law, I would be back to "riding the donkey"! It was a hard decision to make, with serious consequences.

Thirteen years before, at the tender age of nineteen, I had made the decision to serve God, during the bombing of Jerusalem. Some years after that I made another important decision: I pursued my education in philosophy at the risk of losing my faith. (And I almost did—I came very close to dropping either my seminary training or my secular education, because I could not seem to reconcile the two.) A third major decision was when I decided to marry Evelyn for life. I promised she would be my one and only.

Now I was faced with a decision just as serious. Should I continue working at this secular job, or should I quit and serve God full time? The way Evelyn saw it, that decision was already made in 1967 when I promised to serve God. To her, working at a secular company was a detour.

Our dinner with Dr. Bright helped secure the outcome. A few weeks after that meeting, I presented my resignation to the general manager at the airline office. December 31, 1978 would be my last day. I was stepping out in faith.

It had been three years since we had made Jordan our home. We went there feeling defeated; there was nowhere else to go. In those three years God had prospered us and given us many friends and a successful outreach. There was hardly a soul from among the evangelical Christian community that had not heard of us. I knew I could not have done that on my own. Once again, God's finger was in all of it.

In many ways, Evelyn's attitude was correct: My work at the travel agent's office was a detour. But God used that detour to get us where we needed to be. Detours are not necessarily bad; they may take time, but they can be used for our good, and allow us to move forward rather than remain stale. I guess I had wanted to stay in a detour, but of course I know that would not have been a good idea.

Campus Crusade's first step was to send our family to Kenya for six months to train both my wife and me. We met new people, got introduced to a new culture, and benefited tremendously from that experience. The only drawback was having to leave the church that God had allowed us to start before its members had time to grow and mature.

When filling the application to join Campus Crusade, I noted on the application form that I had previous experience in mass communication, specifically radio. I asked for the opportunity to develop that, if possible. The war in Lebanon had forced me to resign, but the work was still in my heart.

It was one of my happiest days in Campus Crusade when my supervisor broke the news that I had been assigned to do the translation, the dubbing and the final production work of the *Jesus* film from English into Arabic. I had done an extensive amount of translation work in Jerusalem, at the seminary, and in Jordan. Our professors at the seminary were mostly English speakers. I was often asked to translate for them during class.

I had to go to a studio in London to produce the Arabic translation. I knew London fairly well, having visited the city numerous times during my work with British Airways.

I also had some experience with the world of audio studios. I could not have chosen a better fit to my skills. It was a perfect match. But it was also an awesome project, a huge responsibility! God gave me grace, and the project was successfully completed. It took seven long weeks.

A year or so after we started with Campus Crusade, the team leader took on a new assignment in another part of the Middle East. I was named the new team leader. The group I was to lead was multicultural and multilingual. I was honored to be given that responsibility, but I lacked the experience.

One of our first goals was getting the approval of the authorities to show the Arabic version of the *Jesus* film in public theaters. We expected the process to be difficult, but thankfully, it was granted without much of a problem. It was a great day to watch it being played in national movie theaters across town. Soon after it appeared, with and without permission, at movie rental stores. It was spreading like wildfire, and we were not going to stop it. We were also beginning to show it at schools, at churches and in homes.

The fact that it was shown in public theaters was big news. But bigger news was yet to come. When the authorities cleared the film for public theaters, they gave permission to show all of it except the very last part, which was an added-on presentation of the gospel to the individual viewer, with a closing at the end to pray to receive Christ. While that part was not to be shown in theaters, there was no such restriction at other locations! This is where the most fascinating responses took place.

Private homes were turned into small theaters as people

invited their friends, colleagues and neighbors. Their small living rooms were filled to capacity and overflowing. Once the lights were turned off, and the film started rolling, a veiled woman here and another there showed up. They did not want to be noticed. They would crouch and watch the film from under the veil!

For almost two hours every eye was glued to the image projected on the wall, in total silence—with some rare but meaningful exceptions. As Christ debates the Sadducees, the viewers are on edge. Who will win the debate? Christ's words are convincing—as convincing to the viewers as they were to the Sadducees. The Sadducees are put to shame, and they turn their backs and leave. The audience breaks the silence in uproarious applause. They lived the moment with Jesus as it was portrayed on the wall before them.

And again, when He calms the waves, they applaud! When he raises Lazarus, they applaud! When He is raised from the dead, they applaud! This is repeated numerous times, and each time the applause is louder than before. The viewers are drawn into the film. They live its events. They have become part of it.

They are also part of it at the site of the crucifixion. This time they do not break the silence with applause, but with sobbing. They had seen all the good that Christ did. They had marveled at each of his miracles. Now they see his body battered, the insults and pain He endures, and finally the nails that pierce his hands and feet. Their emotions build up in them. They would, if they could, save Him from that atrocious death. But they are powerless. They break into tears.

I had shown Christian films before, and translated many

of them for my church in Jerusalem years before. Never had I seen a film produce such an effect on so many people.

What the *Jesus* film seemed to have done was transport the events of two thousand years ago into the present. To many viewers the events were so real they felt like they were living them.

There was no further need to convince anyone of the historical truthfulness of the crucifixion. They saw it with their own eyes. They were personal witnesses of it. You could not convince them otherwise.

Briefly put, the *Jesus* film served as an excellent piece of discipleship, as people lived, even for two short hours, with Christ; as they followed His steps, admired His behavior, reacted to His actions and reactions. That is why it had this tremendous effect on so many of them, irrespective of their religious background.

What happened on a relatively small scale in Jordan was repeated in other countries with larger viewing audiences. In Egypt and Sudan there were similar reports. The power of Christ, even through a film, was being felt in the lives of individuals and societies. There is no telling how many tens of millions viewed the *Jesus* film in North Africa and the Middle East. There is no telling what the lasting effects will be on them or on their societies.

All during our work with Campus Crusade, I longed to be back in radio. There was a uniqueness to its power, a certain flavor and delight to the communication process that went on between me and my audiences, and a secret non-audible communication during those times when silence was more powerful than words. I do not believe in telepathy, but I could sense a certain attachment, almost fondness with my listeners. I was with them in their personal privacy, as they listened in their cars, in their rooms, at their desks, under their bed covers and even in their showers. I was there with them—talking, but also listening and responding. Oh, how I wished to be doing that again!

My desire and longing were only accentuated after a road trip my wife and I took. We were vacationing in the town of Aqaba in the south of Jordan, not far from the Saudi Arabian border. Until that afternoon, I had not considered crossing over.

I knew that the Saudi kingdom did not admit tourists, and I had no business connections that would justify asking for a visa. A visit seemed impossible. Then a friend revealed that he had local government connections and could secure a day's pass into the country.

On a winding two-lane road, flanked by vast stretches of desert on both sides, we entered Saudi Arabia. It was not exactly a vacation trip, not even an extension to our vacation in Aqaba, but it was well worth the time. I wanted to have a sense of penetrating the Saudi Kingdom, even if only for a day.

I had heard from a Catholic young woman, a former colleague at the travel agency, that Saudi Arabia will not even allow pictures of the Virgin Mary to be taken in. She spoke from personal experience. Upon arrival at a Saudi airport, her bag was inspected and the customs agent found a picture of the Virgin Mary. My colleague was told to give it up or she could not be allowed into the country. Despite her religious zeal, she decided she wanted to get in, so she had to let them tear up the picture.

I was not Catholic, so I had no picture of the Virgin Mary on me. In fact, my wife and I made sure we left everything in our hotel room. The only things we had were our car and the clothes on our backs.

The immigration checkpoint and the customs office appeared to be housed in the same building. We arrived, parked our burgundy Nissan and went in. Our day passes were validated and stamped. We were reminded that we had to leave the country that same evening. We thanked them and started making our way toward the door, but we were stopped. Our car was to undergo a search.

I honestly wondered what those customs agents were looking for as they searched our car. Things in Saudi Arabia were much cheaper than in Jordan, so visitors were coming into the country to buy, not sell. Consumer goods, mostly electronics, were plentiful at the small shops in the nearby town.

The sight of the customs agents searching our car did not make much sense to us, especially when they drove it over a pit to search the undercarriage. I suppose they were looking for smuggled goods of some sort. From behind the glass doors we enjoyed the scene, though perplexed over what it was they thought they might find.

If that were not enough to raise our eyebrows, there was more to come. As soon as they finished searching the car from below, they turned their attention to the interior, systematically removing all the seats, front and back. To us it was a futile waste of time—their time and ours. We were not hiding anything. But there was no use complaining. An hour or so later, we got back into our car and drove on.

By the time we made it to the first town, the sun was setting—the time for Muslim prayers. I had heard stories of the Saudi religious police, the Muttawa. Their job was to make people obedient to what the Muslim religion taught about religious observances. Their very name is the Arabic derivative of the word *obey*. That is exactly what we saw them do. The Muslim faithful, especially with such a strict enforcement of the Muslim law, pray five times every day, and one of those times is at sunset.

The small shops were still open. There was not much traffic in that desert town—or for that matter, not much of anything. There were few people on the streets; at one point, only my wife and I remained outside. The religious police were chasing the shopkeepers and their clients with sticks. It was time to pray, and there was no choice but to leave everything and go to the local mosque, or face the consequences. We could see the shopkeepers hesitating; in the end they went, with some leaving the doors to their shops only half closed. It would only take a few minutes and they would be back.

Though small, the shops were loaded with electronic goods. Huge color TV sets, radios and almost anything else electronic was sold there. We spent a few minutes looking, then drove on a few miles past the town. There was nothing, except sand and sea. Finally we stopped by the side of the road and walked by the seaside for a few minutes.

Until that moment, I had not said a word to my wife as to my purpose in taking this trip. Now I felt I had to. It was obvious we had not gone in to buy any goods. We were ready to go back to Aqaba the same way we came, with nothing but our car and the clothes we were wearing. So why did we go in the first place?

Saudi Arabia was on my heart. I wanted to find out how hard it would be to take Bibles in. I was not planning to become a smuggler, but the story my colleague at British Airways told me about the picture of the Virgin Mary left me intrigued. I wanted to see that detailed search procedure for myself. Getting the Bible into Saudi Arabia would be a mammoth task.

I remembered my years in Christian radio, when I had experienced firsthand the challenge of sending Christian Scripture into Saudi Arabia. We had a huge audience, and many hungered to receive the Bible in their own language. But there was no legal way to do it. At the time, we sent very small portions of the Scriptures, and even then listeners were complaining of never receiving the books.

The purpose of my trip to Saudi Arabia was to see whether there was any alternative way to deliver these Scripture portions. To my utter regret there appeared to be none, and I lacked the imagination to come up with a new possibility.

I shared my feelings of desperation with my wife. I also lifted a prayer to the Lord, promising that if He were to give me another opportunity to do radio, I would make it my priority to read the New Testament over the airwaves and challenge my audience to record it. For some reason, I had never thought of that idea until that road trip to Saudi Arabia that afternoon. My longing for radio was as strong as ever— a burning desire. It now had turned to a passion, a prayer and a pledge!

13

More Change

IT HAS BEEN said that the only constant thing in life is change. That was certainly true for our family. Our life resembled to some degree that of nomads. I didn't seem to mind it, and neither did our sons. They were too young to have much of an opinion anyway. But my wife Evelyn, like most women, craved to settle down in a place she could call home.

I was still in my pajamas when the doorbell rang one day in May of 1982, at not quite eight in the morning. My wife and I did not expect any visitors, so I figured it was a neighbor who wanted to borrow something. I answered the door, still in my pajamas. I did not want to keep whoever it was waiting, and since neighbors are almost like family, I wasn't shy about answering the door in my pajamas. But I received an embarrassing surprise that morning!

There at the door were two strange men, foreigners, and the pastor from our church. I invited them in, and immediately excused myself to go and dress. Whatever embarrass-

ment we felt was soon overtaken by that of our visitors, for
coming to see us at such an early hour without advance notice.

The two foreigners were US citizens managing a Christian radio station in Europe. They had come to Jordan to
find an Arabic speaker, any Arabic speaker, who had experience in Christian radio. They were offering me a chance to
go back into Christian radio!

My passion for radio had never died, and in my heart, I
could not wait to jump at the offer. But I could not simply
walk away from what I was doing. Though to me it was a
done deal, my wife and I promised to pray about it and seek
God's guidance in the matter. For a number of months, we
honestly sought God's whisper in our hearts.

On January 1, 1983 we officially joined Trans World Radio. Initially I was to be stationed in Jordan, but in March,
after a three-day visit to the station in Monaco, I was invited
to move there with my family. Our oldest child was ten, and
our youngest was a little over a year.

I sometimes like to meditate on the paths that God has
led *us* over these years. I emphasize the word *us*, because this
is not about me alone, but also my wife, and even to some
extent our sons. In her testimony of how God called her
into full-time Christian ministry, Evelyn always goes back
to God's calling on the life of Abram.

It was those verses in the book of Genesis chapter twelve
that jumped at her. In her late teens she sensed God inviting
her to also leave her country and her father's household. Since
then, she has been back to Egypt for very infrequent and
short visits. The part that she did not quite fully realize at
the time was that in following God's calling, Abram had lived

his life in a tent. He was on the move almost constantly, or so is the general reader's impression.

My wife and I had been married twelve short years and had already made four major moves, as well as half a dozen smaller moves within Jordan itself. Now we were facing still another move, except that this looked more permanent and with much more uprooting than we had experienced thus far.

Jordan was very hospitable to us—and not just us. It was and still is home to several million displaced Palestinians. Jordan has granted most of them nationality, with all its privileges. Jordan opened its doors in 1948 and again in 1967 to floods of Palestinian refugees. In the same way, the civil war of 1975 in Lebanon drove hundreds of thousands from their homes. Once again, Jordan was very hospitable, and many Lebanese found refuge in Jordan.

The same scenario would be repeated after the 1991 Gulf War, and in 2003, as hundreds of thousands of Iraqis found refuge in Jordan. As a family, we have always cherished the kindness and friendship that Jordan offered to us. They will forever be engraved in our memories. Jordan became a home to us in more ways than one. The evangelical Christian community was our family in a true and deep sense.

During my service with British Airways, I had flown to Europe innumerable times, especially London. Every time I boarded the plane to fly back to Jordan, I felt I was going home. But in March 1983, after a brief visit to the Christian station in Europe, I returned with a heavy heart. I had made the trip initially to secure my role in Jordan. I came back with a secure position in Europe.

I did not know how my wife would take the news. I had

signed a contract without calling her and giving her a chance for input. How would I break this news to her?

It was late at night when I arrived home from Europe. At first I tried to act like nothing had changed, but Evelyn sensed something was going on, and she kept asking more questions. In the end, I could not hold back. By midnight, I had told her the whole story.

For the next two weeks we had a very strained relationship. Evelyn did not want to go; she had gotten used to Jordan, and we were well established. The three older boys were in school, and we had plans to build our first house. I was about to take all that away! The move to Europe meant a new beginning for me—a resumption of my love for radio. But for the rest of the family, it was an end—the end of a dream to settle down, to belong!

In the end, as a good Middle Eastern wife, Evelyn gave in. She had spent a lot of time praying, and a lot of time wiping away tears. If *God* were calling me back into radio, she would follow. She worried about our sons growing up in a Western culture. But she was committed to me and to our marriage. That same commitment of hers had always carried us through, and it never wavered in all our years of marriage.

The application for our visa was a long and tedious process. One school year ended and the next one began before the papers finally arrived. Thinking we would be leaving Jordan sooner than we did, we failed to renew the lease on our apartment and suffered the consequences: more moves! Six more within 4 months, to be exact. It was an experience as grueling as all our previous moves put together.

It was not until late September, 1983 that our visas were

finally granted, and my wife, our four sons and I boarded a plane for southern France. We had lived seven years in Jordan. We were now on our way to another country, another continent and a whole new culture. A new page—actually, a new chapter—was being written in our lives.

14

Back to Radio

THE PRINCIPALITY of Monaco, also known as Monte Carlo, is a very beautiful, tiny country tucked in a narrow coastal strip with the azure waters of the Mediterranean Sea on its south side and a number of small French towns on every other side. The chance even to visit, let alone live there, is thought to be a privilege reserved only for the rich. Why and how Trans World Radio established its European headquarters there is a story that belongs in another book. Suffice it to say that this principality, the envy of untold millions of people, was to be our home.

The beauty of the city only added to our cultural adjustment, and probably more so for Evelyn and me than our four sons. We also faced language barriers, including myself, because my French education in Jerusalem had rusted for lack of use. What little I remembered was outdated, bookish French, which was far from the spoken language of Monaco, with its peculiar provincial accent. It was months before I regained some sense of confidence as a French speaker.

Most important, however, was Evelyn's deep sense of up-rootedness, a feeling that would continue to haunt her for years to come.

There was quite a crowd of nationals working at the offices, representing a number of mostly eastern European languages. The Arabic language was also represented; we were the third Arab family unit to join the team. My role at the office was cut out for me; they had even picked out a "radio name" for me—I was told to keep my first name, but change my last. The reason? Security.

Suddenly I found myself plunged into a strange situation. No one had talked of security concerns before, and definitely no one had told me I needed to change my name. I had worked in international radio before, doing basically the same kind of ministry. There were no security concerns then, and I did not have to change my name, even while working out of an Arab country. So why now?

Not long after that I made an equally strange discovery: One of the team members had not been back to the Middle East for years, for fear of retribution—despite the fact that he did not have a voice on the airwaves! It was none of my business, yet I could not help but wonder why.

I knew I could not do that. I could not cut myself off from the audiences I was seeking to reach. I was here to communicate with my people, not to disconnect. We came to serve them better, to engage in their lives on a wider scale than we did the seven years we were in Jordan. Europe was only a launching pad for much broader relationships to the Arab peoples of the Middle East and Northern Africa. To me there was nothing to be afraid of, and definitely nothing to be ashamed of.

I was brought in from Jordan to do two basic jobs: to produce recorded radio programs for later broadcast to the Middle East and/or North Africa; and to engage in the lives of those that write to our mailing address through correspondence.

The station had these general rules in their transmitting policy: Since this was a not-for-profit operation, the microphone could never be used to generate income. Broadcasters could not attack other faiths or other denominations, whether directly or indirectly. The Holy Scriptures were our sole foundation for truth, and they were to be used in a positive manner. Finally, the station was *apolitical*, and did not allow attacks on any political entity. We had no links to any government or political movement, and took every precaution to be viewed that way.

Soon my voice would be on the air again, except more frequently. While working for the Baptist Mission out of Beirut, Lebanon, we had used this same radio station in Europe, but in a very limited way. Usually, not more than fifteen minutes weekly. It was not long before my voice would be carried on the airwaves every day.

The first time I was offered a job in Christian radio, I did not know much about radio or Christianity. I had no training in the art of communication, Christian or otherwise. And I had not had the chance to live out my Christian faith, to test it and have it tested. I had graduated from seminary thinking I had the answers, and I probably did—but they were answers to the wrong questions! I had answers to classroom questions and not necessarily to those that everyday people asked.

Now, twelve years later, things had changed considerably.

I had learned a few things. My past radio experience gave me a certain understanding of what works and what doesn't. My ministry in Egypt and Jordan created a vast reservoir of relational experiences, of direct communication with people, that I could count on. I came to Europe better prepared.

Our brief visit to Saudi Arabia was still very vivid in my memory. I did not forget my prayer or my pledge. And so, at the first occasion, I began reading the New Testament on the air, inviting my audience to record it if they desired to keep a copy. I also offered a hard copy of it to those that asked for one.

There was just one problem: This book was not welcome in many parts of the Middle East and North Africa, and its size in a mailing envelope would often betray it.

Then someone came up with an interesting solution: Divide the book into smaller portions, print it on fine Indian paper, and what you get are a series of booklets we called "skinnies." We had a Skinny Matthew, a Skinny Mark, a Skinny Luke and so on. Getting the whole New Testament into the hands of a seeker now turned into a challenge of keeping track of which 'skinnies' he had received, and which he still needed.

There were other challenges too. The "skinnies" were not heavy duty, and if used regularly, they didn't last long. Moreover, they never drummed up the same respect as the whole New Testament did. And the books of the Old Testament, for the most part, were not published in the same format. That's why most of our audiences asked for the whole Bible, and not a "skinny" part of it.

One such request was made by a girl from Algeria. A regular listener to the Christian broadcasts, she was attracted to the person of Christ and wanted a copy of the Bible. As with others, we started by sending her some "skinnies." At first she was thankful to receive any portion at all. Nevertheless, she kept asking for the whole Bible.

She wanted to know the background to the New Testament portions we were sending her, and she had a lot of questions. A typical letter from this girl was usually several pages long with as many as forty questions. We did what we could to answer her questions, but we could not rewrite the Bible for her, which is basically what many of her questions amounted to. This girl needed a Bible—a complete Bible, in which she could look up the answers for herself.

The first Arabic Bible we sent to her never arrived. We have no clue whether it was censored, stolen, sold, or what. And so, she kept asking. Days turned into weeks. We had to find a way. Finally, I thought that by having a copy sent from another Arab country, the chances of the Bible getting through were far greater. I asked the Bible Society office in Jordan to do that on our behalf.

Three weeks went by. We hoped for the best. But it was not to be. The Bible Society office in Jordan called to say that I could expect a surprise book from them. Soon that book arrived in Europe. It was neatly wrapped, with my name and address written on it. But as soon as I ripped that off, I discovered a second wrapping below, addressed to our listener, using cheap brown paper so as not to attract anyone's attention. But it had not escaped the eagle eye of a post office employee in Algeria. On that brown paper were written the words: "This book is not welcome in Algeria!"

We were really stuck. Other than someone hand-carrying the Bible to her in Algeria, there was nothing we could do.

And of course, it would be foolish to spend the money for such a long trip to carry a single Bible into the country. By then, weeks had turned into months.

The girl was still faithfully listening, and her letters were still coming with the same regularity. The questions changed in nature, but not in number. Every time a different Bible character was presented on radio, her questions would follow. Yet despite all her questions, and all our answers, one small piece was missing in this puzzle: Had she become a follower of Christ, or was she still seeking?

By the time her next letter reached us, many months into this lively correspondence, I had begun to dread her many questions. I could not possibly serve as a Bible dictionary and commentary at the same time. But beyond that, I dreaded her letters because we simply could not meet the one specific need she had always asked for: a copy of the Bible.

Halfheartedly I opened the letter. And there on the first page, on the very first line was one word that lifted my soul for days and weeks, dispelling all my doubts and anxieties: *Hallelujah!* If ever there was a letter from a listener that left an indelible mark on my life, it was that one.

This girl's younger brother attended a boarding school in a French-speaking West African nation. His roommate was a black Christian student, who carried his copy of the New Testament with him to school. As the school term was ending, and the brother was preparing to return home, he asked his roommate if he could borrow the New Testament. The reason? His sister wanted it so badly he could not resist asking for it.

Immediately upon his arrival, and while still at the door, the brother presented the much-wanted book to his sister.

But he made it clear that this was not her copy. He had promised to take it back when school started after the break. Her heart began pounding and her tears started flowing. Finally, she could hold that dear book! It was unbelievable how much she desired it.

In a few minutes she was on her way to the closest bookstore to have each and every page photocopied! She could not allow that book to go back without keeping a copy for herself, even if it was made on a photocopier.

I have since wondered many times how cheaply we have rendered some of the most magnificent words in our Bible, and among them the word *hallelujah*. David and others used it extensively in Scripture, especially in the book of Psalms, but each and every time it was used, there was a major breakthrough, nothing short of what this Algerian girl experienced.

Feelings of relief overtook my soul. I realized that was only the New Testament, and that it was in French and not in the Arabic language. So be it. At least she had that to work with. Little did I realize at the time that her letters full of questions would continue for many years to come. They would be different, but just as many and just as important to her. My soul was overjoyed that this girl had become a follower of Christ. She proved to be a dedicated follower who took her faith very seriously.

It was marvelous to see God at work. Where we had reached a total roadblock, God was at work, using someone as close as her brother. Seeking to send her a Bible, we had not left any stone unturned, yet we had failed. To God, the answer was right at her side. She had realized that too. She could not have made a more fitting statement than the one she did: *Hallelujah!* That said it all, in one simple word. She gave praise to the One to whom praise was due!

Judging by the numbers of letters we received, Algeria was one of three Arab countries where we seemed to enjoy a good-sized audience. The other two were Egypt and Iraq, with Egypt always leading but Iraq a close second. The Iraqi letters also stood out by the colorful stamps the listeners used. They were mostly of the now-deposed Iraqi leader Saddam Hussein, each time dressed up differently. My small collection dating back to the mid-1980s leaves no doubt as to who reigned supreme in Baghdad back then.

Our team at the radio station took their job very seriously. Each letter mattered—each letter we *received*, that is. Every once in a while, a listener would complain that he or she had sent their second, third, or at times tenth letter, and did not hear back! To us, it was their first. Was that a trick used by some of them to put pressure on us to deliver what they asked for? Or was it true? And if so, why?

In reality, we had no reason to doubt the sincerity of these letters. Many of the writers did not want anything but an answer to a pressing question. We always apologized, and followed that by explaining that what we held in our hands was only the first letter ever received from them. Soon we discovered a similarly challenging situation: Some of our listeners were not receiving our letters. The problem existed on both sides of the correspondence process.

15

Challenges that Stretch

A S USUAL, the stamps from Iraq were colorful. Also as usual, the stamps depicted the Iraqi leader with his attractive colorful apparel. The contents of one letter were not as colorful. They were graphic, but the shades were dark and somber.

This one letter stood out, not for its depiction of the glory of radio, or the magnificence of correspondence, but of the limitations of both. It might as well have been written with the blood and tears of the young girl that penned it.

Her situation was very personal—too personal! According to her testimony, no one else knew her story except God, herself, and now me, the person to whom she wrote her letter. Those words carried with them the weight of a huge responsibility. She could have written to any number of radio speakers. To pick me from among them was both an honor, and given her situation, a dire and difficult challenge.

Our listeners always found it easier to write about their personal challenges and problems to someone living abroad, far away from where they lived, in order to avoid shame. That was true especially of girls, and true even when the person writing is not the guilty party. Being the victim of sexual assault, for example, is something a girl would go to any length to avoid revealing to someone close by.

The girl who wrote this letter was a victim of rape as a child. The assailant: Her brother! For many years she had kept the secret to herself. Her own mother could not be trusted with it, not when the culprit is her son. Sharing that secret with her dad was completely out of the question. Such audacity could have put her very life at risk. (To absolve shame in the family and larger society, some practice "honor killings"—murdering the victim to eliminate the shameful situation.)

To make matters worse, she was now in her late teens, and her cousin was asking for her hand in marriage. He was certain to discover on their wedding night that she was not a virgin. Where on earth could this girl turn for counsel? Middle Eastern boys can lose their virginity and no one seems to care. But not girls!

Knowing the shame that she and her family would face if she were to get married, this girl wondered what she should do. Should she make a vow to become a nun to avoid marriage? Was there a way to repair the damage? The damage to her soul seemed beyond repair. She only wanted a way out of this impasse—anything!

It was not unusual for me to wait a few days before I answered a listener's questions. But this letter was too urgent. I lifted my heart to God, asked for His guidance and took time the same day to write back a five-page letter. I pleaded with her to speak to her mother. If anybody could understand her plight as a female in a society where males were kings, it would be her mother. If that were not an option, she should seek out someone locally as a spiritual guide.

The idea of speaking to this girl over the airwaves did not cross my mind. Discussing such matters in the mid-1980s was taboo. The letter was far too graphic for a conservative audience. And most importantly, I did not want to put her in jeopardy.

The letters kept coming. Every new day carried new letters to us by the score. Every day, I waited to hear from this girl. I was very concerned. I did not want her to pay for her brother's crime. I had done my part; all I could do now was wait and hope and pray for the best.

During those weeks I took a special interest in the letters from Iraq, sorting them out of each morning's mail and opening them first. Three weeks went by, and then it came—not the letter I wanted, nor from the person I was expecting to hear from! The letter came from her cousin, a girl about her same age. It was a letter I never wanted to see!

I never read such cussing in my life as I did on those pages. She said I was the most awful thing that ever happened to the human race. I was given every name in the book, and more. My sin, according to this cousin, was that I did not care enough to answer the girl's letter—and as a result, the bride-to-be had killed herself. The weight of shame was so heavy on her, she preferred to die.

For both her shame and suicide, I was partly to blame. My skill in communicating Christian truths, that same skill which initially generated her letter to me, became the judgment bench! That day I realized that radio messages can give people life, but they can also kill!

Radio is an excellent tool of communication. It has been proven again and again. But it has its limitations. It cannot be all things to all people. In radio we are trained to create presence as we seek to communicate. We are trained to ride in people's cars as we speak to them; as we whisper in their ears, as we touch them and keep them company. Obviously there are very real limits to the amount of presence one can create; it is at best virtual, not real. When faced with a challenge like sending a Bible to Algeria, or counseling a hopeless Iraqi girl, radio becomes just words—empty words!

It is interesting to note from Scripture that God's ultimate means of communicating to man, according to the first chapter of the Gospel of John, was to send His Word, Jesus Christ of Nazareth. Jesus was not an empty word. He was the Word Incarnate. He was the Word that became flesh.

The limitations of our words carried by radio are a challenge that has haunted me many times in my Christian radio career. Or, as an old friend said to me once, "You have put God in a box"—the box being the radio. To him, the real issue was one of presence, of incarnation. To us, the issue was proclamation. Looking back, I am convinced that the real tragedy was that these two tracks had worked separately for too long. Those that paid the price were the people on the ground!

Thankfully, not every letter presented such difficult and challenging situations. There were good days, too, when we received every single letter a listener sent us, and he or she received what we sent them. Such was the testimony of a mother of three from North Africa. (Most of our mail came from young singles, an age group which is seeking different perspective on life; it was unusual to receive letters from married women.)

The letter from this mother carried a most marvelous testimony. Her oldest was fifteen; her youngest ten. She had lost her husband some years before. Since remarriage was out of the question, she devoted all her time to her job and her kids, and listened to our Christian broadcasts late in the evening. According to her testimony, she took notes of the Bible exposition messages that were presented daily, and the next morning took the time to share those with her kids!

Letters like these kept us going day in and day out. Letters like these renewed our strength and our vision, reminding us that our work was not in vain, but was paying dividends for eternity!

Women, to a large degree, were the forgotten segment of Arab society in terms of missionary work. In the early part of the twentieth century, a few mission agencies to North Africa recognized the key role that women played in the Arab home, and thus sought to bring the gospel to them. With the huge population growth that followed, the emphasis shifted. There were more young boys and girls than women, and they were easier to reach. Outreach to women began to fall by the wayside.

Contrary to current prevalent images of male dominance in the Middle Eastern society, wives and women are the true keys to their homes, rather than husbands and fathers. Men exercise influence outside the home, but within its walls, women continue to play a major, though hidden, role. They broker the peace with in-laws and neighbors, and have a much larger influence on their children than men are willing to admit. If present-day missions have failed to win the

Arab society at large, it is because we have failed to use the proper key to get in!

There is no doubt that the age bracket in the Arab world is increasingly young. There is also no doubt that it is much easier to reach the *young and restless* than women. We have more contacts and more ways to reach them, especially since most of them are educated, while the older generation, especially among women, is not. Planting shrubs is easier than planting trees, but the branches of a tree reach farther than a shrub. Adult women of the Arab world are like trees; they can influence their husbands, children and society to a much greater degree than all the youth put together.

By the early 1990s God allowed us to grow and expand. Our vision was being shaped by events taking place in other countries and continents. Soon after the demise of the Soviet Union, and especially after the fall of the Berlin Wall, there was a sense that God was about to move mightily in the Middle East. We wanted to have a presence not only on the radio dial, but also on the ground.

Soon we had offices in a number of countries, and our Arabic staff multiplied in number several times over. With that expansion, much of what we carried out in Europe was transported to those countries. The bulk of our programs was now produced locally and with that the correspondence with our listeners.

The audience was no longer invited to write principally to a box office address in Europe. The creation of production centers in the Middle East introduced a huge number of local addresses that were much closer to the audience, and the number of incoming letters multiplied fifty times over.

The new centers also began publicizing fax and phone

numbers. The fax numbers were provided for those in more affluent societies of the Arabian Gulf, so they could send a fax one day and expect an answer the next. The phone numbers were for those who needed to talk to someone, and also for the huge proportion of listeners who could not read or write.

Omar lived in Algeria and was twenty-two years old. He left school as a teenager to avoid getting caught up in politics: all his classmates sided either with the government or the Islamic fundamentalists. Civil war was ravaging the country with no end in sight. Tens of thousands had died, and Omar and untold millions were taken hostage.

The economy was in a shambles; more than half the population had lost their jobs, and Omar's father could barely support them. Omar decided to open a small shop selling trinkets. During the night hours, he spent his time listening to the radio. The government stations were always reporting on the war, and Omar was sick of it. While looking for something different to listen to, he came upon a Christian station.

His schooling, though limited, allowed him to read and write. So he began writing to an address in France. The station generated questions in his mind, questions about the Christian faith and about life in general. For a year or more, Omar faithfully corresponded with the center and the center with him. The letters were slow both ways, but they were not interrupted. The broadcasts and letters kept him alive; they were his only hope for a better future.

Before long, Omar invited a friend to listen with him, then a second, then a third! Within months a group of five young men, roughly the same age as Omar, were crammed into his small room and huddled around his transistor radio, listening. At the end of the transmission every night, the five would spend an extra hour or two discussing what they had heard.

Around that same time, one of the production centers in the Middle East started advertising international phone numbers. One of their regular callers was Omar. He spent much of his income on international calls. He needed to talk to someone.

Then one day two young men showed up at one of our Middle East offices. Both looked famished; their skin was scorched and their eyes were sunken in their sockets. I stood up to greet them as they were introduced to me. The name of one rang a bell. It was Omar! I had heard reports about his regular, sometimes frantic, telephone calls, but I never expected that one day I would meet him, and definitely not at this location—about two thousand miles from Algeria! I asked how he had found his way here, and this is the story he told me.

The five young men continued to come together to listen to the Christian broadcasts and discuss what they heard. Because Omar was the oldest among them, was the first to listen and had the boldness to invite the others to listen to Christian broadcasts in his home, the group elected Omar as their leader.

Not long after, Omar's family discovered what was going on, threw him out and told him never to come back. They were afraid his activities would bring retaliation from the Islamic fundamentalists, and they were right.

No sooner had he left his home than the others were forced to join him, living as nomads, with the fundamentalists at their heels. Soon the extremists got hold of one of them and slit his throat. A few months later they captured a second young man of the group, then a third, and they shared the same fate as the first. By that time, Omar's telephone calls to the Middle Eastern office became quite hysterical. He wanted out, and he wanted out *now*!

We, however, did not know how to deal with their situation. Our production and correspondence offices were never meant to be refugee centers. None of the team members, including myself, was trained in how to deal with such crises. Even the local churches had not faced such situations, at least not in their recent history, and were hesitant to get involved in such a high-profile, risky activity as a ministry to converts from Islam. We were all very ill-prepared.

So Omar and his remaining companion were on their own. They fled from town to town seeking refuge, completely destitute and their lives in constant danger. But they did not lack ingenuity. They set their minds on making the trip to our offices, come what may. For a whole month they traveled on buses, trains, trucks, a boat, and for quite a distance, especially when they crossed country borders, on foot. They endured hunger, sickness and fatigue. When I met them, they had just arrived, one day earlier!

Omar was now twenty-five; he had started this journey of faith three years before. At the onset, he had no clue where that journey would lead him—that was part of the "faith" element. Before me was a giant, though in stature he was quite small. For the first time, I realized what it can cost someone to become a follower of Christ. Omar had lost his family, friends and country. Three of his companions had lost their lives! All of that they deemed of less worth than following Christ.

Meeting Omar and his remaining companion stretched me in all kinds of directions. It also stretched the ministry I represented and supervised. Before me was a live example of putting our money where our mouth was. Until then, the focus of our work was on radio—nothing but talk. Call it Bible studies, sermons, whatever you wish, in the end it was mere talk—nothing more, nothing less!

Even the extension of that talk was just words, whether in a letter to a listener or in a booklet. More talk! And we were experts in words and talk. We had invented systems to deliver them in an effective, efficient, and timely manner. But that did not change their nature. They were still words— talk, talk and more talk!

Now before me, all that talk had turned into lives—the lives of Omar and his companion, and even the spent lives of the three that were now missing! I had wanted to connect our talk on the airwaves with something more tangible on the ground. But, honestly speaking, this was not what I was expecting, not so abruptly! I felt we had been catapulted into this without any preparation or training.

Our friends soon discovered that we were not prepared, and not just financially. In fact, the financial component was the easiest to overcome. But what about security? What about legal status? While we're at it, why not throw in employment, marriage and a host of other major issues?

Our friends thought they had the answer: perhaps we could help them secure a visa to a European country that would be willing to give them religious asylum. Easier said than done! The country they had in mind was already bulging at the seams with North African immigrants. They did not want more, whether for religious asylum or otherwise!

We tried, nonetheless, but as expected, we failed. Our office would have to find some other way to deal with this emerging situation, and learn through the process.

The experience of our friends from Algeria stretched us all—probably more so me than others, because I was the one most responsible for the new approach to our regional work which developed over the next several years.

16

A Wanted Man

IT HAD been twenty years since I had produced my first Christian radio program with little understanding of what was involved in the art of doing radio. For many long years my voice was being heard every single day. For as many long years my handwriting was not a secret, when my pen scripted innumerable letters answering my audience's questions.

That was now a thing of the past. Others were carrying on the program production and listener correspondence. My role had changed almost completely. Now I was strategizing, drawing the bigger picture, and training others, helping them develop their skills in every aspect of the work. With new responsibilities came new challenges, and the Algerian experience was one of them. But there was more in the making!

My new responsibility at the Christian radio station meant more trips, mostly to Arab countries. That had been my region of responsibility when I produced programs, as well as now. I never overstayed my need to be in a given country. There was never time for sightseeing or tourism. I was there with a single-minded purpose. Once my business was finished, which never exceeded a few days, I would be out—or so I thought.

There were no signs of trouble at the port of entry. As usual, I was made to wait half an hour to an hour on a wooden bench in the large hall. As usual, my Arab passport was taken away for further investigation. I didn't quite know what the security office was looking for. Every trip it was the same routine, except that sometimes they would call me into a small side office for personal interrogation.

Thankfully, I was not in this alone. Others of diverse nationalities were also made to wait. An officer came out carrying a stack of passports and official documents in his hand, and started calling out names, including mine. Fortunately, there would be no interrogation this time. I was handed my passport and soon found my way to the exit.

I spent the morning with our team. In the afternoon our ministry country coordinator and I were going over some business issues when he was suddenly called out. He returned a few minutes later with a newspaper under his arm. He did not sit back at his desk. With a serious and worried look on his face, he asked me to step out with him, saying we had some important business to take care of.

I stood up and left the room with him, wondering what was going on. Hurriedly, he opened the newspaper to the front page. There in big bold letters was an eye-catching title: *Plot to Ignite Religious War Uncovered!* The plotter: *Hanna Labib* (*My radio name*)! There was no mistaking it. My full name was there, and the work I did. Included in this breaking news report was the text of a letter I was accused of writing—a letter I had never seen before!

At that instant I was reminded of the colleague who had worked for the station in Europe—the same colleague who had fears of returning to his country lest he be summoned by the authorities. Back then, his statements took me by surprise. I could not understand his fears, especially since he did not have any presence on the air. I was in his country now; maybe he was right after all!

I wondered what was going on. Why now? My presence on the radio had been reduced to a minimum. Now I was seldom heard. As to answering listeners' letters, I was doing practically none of that. I was not plotting anything against anyone. I was innocent of this accusation!

That was no time for such a mental exercise. The best course of action, according to my colleague, was to leave as quickly as possible before word spread. We had to arrive at the travel agent before the offices closed. It was nearly four in the afternoon; there was no time to lose.

Changing the ticket to the earliest possible flight cost me six hundred US dollars. I would be departing at five the next morning. I had to spend one more night in that city.

I walked back to my hotel with a very divided and heavy heart. Part of me did not want to leave. I did not want to run away. Where was my faith, and what example was I leaving behind?

The other part of me could not wait to get out. Since there was no truth to the accusations against me, and since the newspaper falsely portrayed me as the author of a letter I never wrote, then obviously I could not expect much justice in a court of law. I knew I better leave.

I lay on my bed and closed my eyes. I did not even bother to get undressed. I needed to be up at two in the morning;

keeping my clothes on would save time. Besides, what if a security agent came to get me? I did not want to have to nervously put my clothes on.

My eyes were closed, but I could not sleep. I was just plain scared. I had not had any dinner and not much for lunch. An empty stomach seems to leave more room for butterflies in one's stomach! I tossed and turned, frequently stealing looks at the door, listening for any approaching noise. There was nothing but silence—which made me all the more apprehensive.

By two the next morning I was on my feet and down in the lobby. There were always taxis waiting outside. The drivers would many times spend the night chatting with the security agents at the hotel doors. I settled my bill, got out and grabbed a taxi. Usually I haggled and dickered, but not that morning. I was happy to pay anything the driver asked. I wanted out at any price.

Checking in at the airport was fairly simple. What I had qualms about was the passport check. This was the moment: If the authorities were going to stop me from leaving, that would be the time to do it. I was nervous as I approached the officer. He looked at the photo, then looked up at me. Within seconds he handed me back my passport and wished me a safe trip. I thanked him and swiftly moved away.

It was still two hours before boarding, and two and a half hours before the flight would take off. I had at least that much time to continue to be scared. The security agents could still come and get me. As it was, even after I boarded the plane and it took off, I still worried they would call the plane back since it would be in the national airspace for another forty minutes or so. My fears had taken over.

As a churchgoing Christian, I had learned the principles. As a pastor and teacher, I had taught them to others. I knew quite well that fear was not of faith or of love. Love and faith come together as an amalgam and produce trust or hope. Did I have faith that God loved me? Yes—in my head I did! Where was my faith that day? Why couldn't I trust God? Was He the God of the good times, but not of the bad? But then, why do I even need a God during the good times? Is this the reason why affluent societies tend to become more secular?

I had never known fear like I did then. Yet it seemed I needed to learn my lesson another way. When I met the two Algerian boys, Omar and his colleague, I thought the best I could offer was to pay their way back to their home country. To fly them back! In my little mind, I thought I was doing the Kingdom a service. I was convinced they needed to stay the course come what may. In my mind, I was convinced they were called to be salt and light to their own countrymen. Their answer that day silenced me, though it didn't convince me: They said I was asking them to commit suicide!

How preachy can a preacher become? I guess too much! I know I was that day. But not anymore! I had learned my lesson. Fear was not of God, but fear is human. I was human, and I was afraid, very afraid! It is obvious that I will remain human and as such can still face situations when fear could grip my heart again in the same way.

In seeking to reach out to my Muslim brothers and friends, I had learned a very important lesson about how they prioritize their belief systems and their practices. As a Christian, my belief system comes first, and my practices are always secondary. This influences my approach to ministry in general. One of the first things I have learned to do, as was done with me, was cover the basics. My theology had to be right.

Going back to my Christian journey of thirty some years ago, this is how it all started. The challenge I faced with my Catholic catechism was about a belief system. It was not about Christian practices. The Catholic nuns at the orphanage in Bethany lived a sacrificial and exemplary life. My Catholic teachers, the monks that ran the day school, lived an impeccable life. They were completely above reproach. But I got fixed on the theological side of things. I wanted to have a solid Biblical foundation. I was interested in what I could learn in class.

My Muslim brothers and friends have since taught me a great deal about how and why they do what they do. To them practice comes first. It is their practice that carries their faith. This is not to say that they do not have their theology. They definitely do. However, their practices are the foundation. To be a Muslim, you have to exercise a certain number of duties. Prayer is one, fasting during the month of Ramadan is another, and there are others.

In Christianity, at least in evangelical Christianity, it seems like the most important part is to have your theology correct. What you do after that seems to make some, but not much, difference. I am always amazed when I attend a baptismal service for adults. The baptizer seems always hung up on issues of theology. His questions to the person being baptized mostly revolve around such issues.

I am watching and waiting to find out how it is that the life of the person being baptized has changed. What has his newfound faith changed in his lifestyle? How has it changed his values? Was he a money monger and now gives his money to the poor? Where are the changes that look like the ones that happened to Matthew the tax collector, or to Zacchaeus, or many others in Scripture?

For one reason or another, we have shifted the emphasis from a changed life to a changed theology. We do this either in total ignorance of what the Gospels present to us, or in total defiance of it. In His encounters with everyday people, Jesus did not ask about their theology. What He did was give them new life: "Go and sin no more!"

How has this shift in emphasis affected Christianity? Is there any room for self-criticism? Could it be that our permissive societies, our liberal views and our moral laxity were born out of our emphasis on theological correctness rather than the testimony of a changed life!

In seminary I graduated with the highest honors. I thought I had all the answers, though everyone else knew I didn't. That day in the Middle East, with fear gripping my heart and mind, I made a huge discovery: I discovered that I was still in class. I still had years ahead of me, and would probably never graduate. I thought I had the answers. Now I know I didn't have the right questions. My answers were made in a seminary classroom, in a church sanctuary. But the real questions were made in the battlefield, a place in which I had little experience until that day.

Once back home, I had all the time in the world to reflect on my latest experience on the field. It was far from glorious. It helped pull my feet down to the ground. I tend by nature to be more of an idealist than a realist. My strategies did not leave much room for possible holes in them. That is what I had thought. I came to discover that was as far from the truth as could be.

That experience also changed my preaching, at least for a time. As an idealist, I also tended to be judgmental. Things were always in two colors: black or white. Although I do not qualify as a pessimist, yet in the Sunday school class that I taught when I was in town, as well as in the sermons I preached, I always sensed a certain tendency to correct my hearers about something. That also was beginning to change.

17

Abundant Grace

OUR CHURCH congregation in Monaco was relatively
small. It was mostly made up of our staff family and a
very few individuals from the community. We leased the
auditorium from the French *Église Reformée* (Reformed
Church). Their church building was situated next door to
our offices. Our staff pastor served the English-speaking community at large, but gave his time primarily to our team.

Like other US-sent missionaries, our staff pastor went
home on furlough every two years. This he did during the
summer months. But the church services did not stop. Sunday school as well as the Sunday worship service went on as
usual. Ordained ministers and non-ordained missionaries
took turns filling the pulpit during his absence. I was asked
and had signed up to do it that week.

It was a sunny Saturday afternoon on the French Riviera
that July weekend. I couldn't take advantage of it. I was home
preparing the Sunday morning message, and keeping an eye
on our boys. Evelyn went out for coffee with one of our staff

women. Coffeehouses were everywhere. The one that Evelyn especially liked to go to was the Café de Paris, adjacent to the famous Monte Carlo Casinos.

It was still light when Evelyn came back. She had been out three hours or so. She was barely inside the door when she cried out, "Guess who is in town!" Evelyn knew very well that I never liked guessing. I knew she wouldn't be able to keep her secret very long. I waited, and seconds later the answer came: "Be ready to preach to Dr. Billy Graham to-morrow. He's in town. We ran into him a few minutes ago. Rather, he ran into us."

Evelyn and her friend had finished sipping their coffee, chatting and watching the passersby, especially the neatly dressed Italians that visited town on weekends. The short way back home goes past one of the city's best streets for window shopping. Boulevard des Moulins had the most ex-quisite stores in town, and window shopping, whether for clothing, jewelry or a seaside apartment, was a familiar pas-time along that small street. Evelyn and her friend probably spent as much time walking back as they did sitting at the café. And of course they continued chatting.

Suddenly, someone laid his hands on their shoulders. They turned back. Someone else had been listening in, especially to the very last bit of their conversation. To their complete amazement, it was Dr. Billy Graham.

We had seen Dr. Graham in previous years. We knew he was writing his memoirs, and had chosen the quiet Princi-pality of Monaco to do that. For a few summers in a row, he would come for two or three weeks. He usually showed up at our small church on Sunday morning unannounced. He would come, take a seat, possibly lift up a public prayer and listen like everyone else to the preaching of the Word. On rare occasions he would stand up to share a minute or two about his ministry and what God was doing in and through him.

I heard what Evelyn said and sank in my seat. My mind raced. I was not about to preach to Dr. Graham, not in a thousand years. Suddenly I had an idea—an ingenious idea!

I ran to the phone. I called the station manager, Paul Semenchuck. Paul was from Russia. He'd been in Monaco much longer than we had. I had no idea how to get hold of Dr. Graham, but I was sure Paul had ways of reaching him. If only I could talk him into inviting Dr. Graham to preach, that would kill two birds with one stone! It would give our small church family the unique honor of having Dr. Graham address us, and just as importantly, it would save me the embarrassment of preaching with him in the audience! And if Paul did not succeed in convincing Dr. Graham to preach, he might as well do it himself.

Paul heard my pleas. But he was adamant: When Dr. Graham comes to town, he comes to write his memoirs, not to preach, he said. They had tried to have him speak before, and he had always declined. He was happy to come and listen. And no, Paul would not preach for me.

I was in a corner; there was no getting out of this. I was very nervous. In my mind I knew it was about presenting God's Word and not about who was in your audience. That was merely good theory! In reality, this is not how it works. Your audience makes a huge difference. I know it did for me!

The next morning we were all in church: my wife, our four sons and I. A few minutes before the service began, Dr.

and Mrs. Graham arrived. They were met at the door and seated. All around our small sanctuary there were audible whispers. The eyes were on our special guests.

I felt completely out of place. I had never dreamed of delivering a sermon to such noble guests. How could a small Palestinian boy preach to the greatest evangelist of all time? I was not worthy of such honor.

I still was not convinced I could do it. The singing over, I was invited to the platform. Before I could climb the two or three steps, I turned to Dr. Graham and said that my heart's desire was to be in his place and he in mine. He smiled and said, "I have come to hear you!"

My heart sank within me. That was it. I had preached hundreds of times on radio and in person, in various situations and occasions. But that morning it seemed I was presenting my very first message to the class at the seminary— and hoping for a passing grade!

I had prepared a message on a unique passage in the New Testament. It was unlike other passages because in that story we hear of the Lord Jesus touching a blind person two times instead of once. Normally it was enough for the Lord to say a word to bring about healing. It was enough for someone to touch Him also once to get healing. In my study I had found it intriguing as to why the Lord would touch someone twice, with the blind man not receiving complete healing the first time around. I titled my message "The Second Touch."

I was very aware of my accent. After all, English is not my native language. I forced a smile on my face in an effort to hide my nervousness and did my best to keep my attention on my notes. I wanted to make sure I did not go out of the subject. This was not about finishing on time. It was about finishing. The song leader was left to close in prayer.

Many things had changed in me and in my preaching over the years. Many things except one: my timidity! If it were up to me, once I finished preaching I would be the first one out the door and on my way home. Shaking people's hands at the end of the service has never been one of my favorite activities. I had learned the words worshipers say to the preacher by heart, and I have no clue what is sincere and what is not.

The one phrase that has always baffled me was, "God bless you!" I still wonder what most people mean when they say that to a preacher. It is not likely they mean for God to multiply him, especially not the length of his Sunday messages! What exactly do they mean? There are no conclusive answers.

So here I was at the door. Standing in line to shake my hand were Dr. and Mrs. Graham. My mind started racing again. I didn't know what they were going to say, and more importantly, I didn't know what I could say to them. I was prepared for one more "God bless you," but it did not come. Instead, Dr. Graham said to me that God had spoken to him.

I was dumbfounded. How do I answer him? I knew I shouldn't take him too seriously, and I didn't. I also knew I shouldn't take myself too seriously. I smiled, shook his hand and repeated what I had said to him before I preached. I really meant it. My place was in the pew, not on the platform with him in the pew.

Dr. Graham probably read my mind. He probably knew the thoughts and tensions that were building up in me when he said that God had spoken to him through me. He also knew that I did not take his words too seriously. He was still standing holding my hand. I felt so small, both in stature and in size. I am five foot seven, and he is over six feet tall. Looking intently at me he said again: "I really mean it. God spoke to me." If his first statement took me by surprise, his second shocked me.

It was about ten the next morning when the station manager called me into his office. He asked me if I knew whether someone recorded the message the day before. Normally they did. I was curious and asked why. His answer was very brief and to the point: Dr. Graham wanted a cassette copy.

I had thought that the embarrassing experience the day before was behind me. Sunday was over and this was the beginning of a new work week. Wanting to avoid further follow-up on this subject, I said I will look into the matter. That was Monday. I expected the matter to be completely out of everybody's mind before the week was over. Not so.

Wednesday morning I was called one more time to the station manager's office. He asked whether I was successful in getting a cassette copy. I told him that the Sunday service was definitely not recorded. For once I was glad it was not. One more time, I asked why he was pressing the issue. One more time he said, "Dr. Graham called again." He added, "He says if they did not record your message, he would like to have a copy of your notes, with your permission to use them."

This time I was totally overwhelmed. I had no more reason to doubt Dr. Graham's earlier comments to me as he shook my hand. I went back to my office, got out my Bible, and spent the next hour cleaning up my notes before giving them to Paul to pass on to Dr. Graham.

Back in my office, I shut my door, closed my eyes and wept. I was completely awestruck by God's goodness to me. His grace had been overabundant. Why He would choose a nobody from the dark alleys of the old city of Jerusalem, and give him such grace, was humanly inexplicable. I did not do anything to deserve this. It was God's grace—God's grace plus nothing!

God did not need to prove anything to anyone, much less to me. He does not owe anybody anything. And yet, exactly one year later, Dr. Graham came to town again. And again I was assigned to preach. Again I pleaded to get out of it, but to no avail. It was too much to ask me to preach with Dr. Graham in the audience a second time! But no—it had to happen again.

Except that this time around, Dr. and Mrs. Graham had been invited, along with my wife Evelyn and I, for a meal at a colleague's home that afternoon. God wanted to deepen my sense of His grace. He knew I was thick-skulled and probably needed to see His hand two times in a row to understand!

18

Followers of Christ, But Not "Christians"

I WANT to share the stories of several people whom I have met in my travels, people who have become followers of Christ and have trusted Him for forgiveness of their sins, yet do not call themselves "Christians," with all the cultural and political baggage that this term carries with it in the Middle East.

Cornelius

With the expansion of the Arabic ministry via radio, there was a growing need to train new producers. With twenty years or more in my background as radio programmer and producer, and with the need to do the training in Arabic, I stepped in to fill that role.

Part of the plan included adapting the language to be as close as possible to what is used on the street. This is not as simple a process as one might think, because the Arabic language has a large number of different dialects.

The Arab world consists of over twenty independent countries, each with one or more distinct dialects. Egypt boasts the largest population in the Arab world, and its dialect is most widely understood, so we used Egyptian quite a bit in our broadcasts. We also carried programs in Moroccan, Lebanese, Palestinian and many other dialects. One dialect that was still missing on our dial was Northern Sudanese. I was therefore pleased to discover that a good number of Sudanese students were attending seminary in Lebanon.

I made the trip to the Beirut, Lebanon seminary where Evelyn and I had received our theological training twenty-five years before. When we attended, not a single student was from Sudan; now there were fourteen or more. The director granted me permission to conduct on-campus training in basic principles of oral communication and writing for radio. The week-long training course was held in the afternoons, following the regular morning classes. One afternoon we had an uninvited guest, a young Lebanese man.

Moussa was probably in his mid-twenties. He did not seem very interested in the class, but as we closed that session he came to ask a favor. He asked me to meet with his future in-laws, especially the father. My afternoons were full, and my evenings were occupied—more importantly, I didn't even know this young man or his in-laws-to-be! But Moussa was persistent.

Although I had lived in Beirut many years before, I didn't know the part of town to which I was being driven, much less what to expect. It was nearly ten at night, not exactly a time to visit total strangers. I promised myself it would be a short visit.

As we walked from the car toward one of the apartment buildings, I could see the silhouettes of two men on the balcony of the first floor. I could also hear them speaking; it was a quiet neighborhood, and they were quite loud. "Here they come," said the one, and they disappeared in the darkness of the stairwell.

Halfway up the stairs these men met us. One of them, a tall, burly fellow, wrapped his arms around me, lifted me off the ground and showered me with kisses on both cheeks—one, two, three, four and counting! Having lived in Europe for fifteen years or so, the Arabic custom of men kissing each other was becoming foreign to me, and it made me feel a little uneasy. But I reminded myself that I was back home in the Middle East, where that friendly habit persists.

I was led into a home, met and welcomed by what I imagined was the wife and three daughters of this tall fellow. I was not yet seated when the man of the house said, "I am Cornelius, and you are Peter. The only difference," he added, "is that I am already saved." A three-minute radio talk presented eight years before had challenged this man and brought him to his knees.

I have been told by experts in the field of communication that radio is good at disseminating information, and somewhat good at entertaining an audience (though far less than it used to be before the advent of television). But persuasion—convincing someone to buy an advertised product, or convincing someone to believe in Christ and follow Him—is not, we are told, one of radio's strengths.

Such statements can only cast doubt on the value of radio to bring about a turning point in someone's life. And yet, obviously, that was not the experience of our friend

"Cornelius." It was not the experience of Omar, and hundreds of others who did come to faith by the simple means of Christian radio.

"Cornelius" had heard one of my daily three-minute programs from years ago in which I had asked the question, "Who crucified Jesus?" Even for those among the Arab people who deny His crucifixion, the idea of blaming the Jewish people for Jesus' death is a readily available answer. My talk was redressing that, basically placing the moral and spiritual responsibility on all of us, Arabs included.

One cannot say much in three minutes, but when the Spirit of God is at work, one does not need much time. A listener does not need more than three minutes to be personally convicted of his role in that crucifixion. In his personal testimony that night, this man "Cornelius" said he was driven to his knees, confessed his sins and accepted by faith the forgiveness that Christ offered. In the eight years that had passed, he had witnessed of that new life to his relatives, and twelve members of his family had also come to faith and were now followers of Jesus.

Radio experts may be correct after all: Radio is probably not the best means of persuasion. In my experience in Christian radio to the Middle East and North Africa, I like to think of us drawing on the Presence and power of God's Holy Spirit to persuade and present people to Christ. "Cornelius" was one of those.

Sammy

God never ceases to surprise us. In many ways our audiences have the ability to do that too. It is worth noting that few of our listeners realized that we did not do live broadcasting—that we were not on site when our programs were being aired. Our programs were usually taped two or three weeks before they were aired. When our Middle East audiences tuned in, many of us were probably sound asleep; the programs were broadcast at a very late evening hour.

It was past midnight when the phone in our apartment rang. We were all in bed; our sons had school the next morning, and my wife and I had a busy day ahead of us. Who could it be? Was it an emergency? My wife's relatives lived in the USA; mine were still in the old country. If it was an emergency, there was not much we could do at that late hour. My wife and I hesitated for a moment, wondering whether we should let it ring until the caller gave up. Finally, afraid the ringing would wake our boys, I picked up the receiver.

"Hello brother Hanna. I am Sammy," came the voice from the other end. I had a cousin living in Jordan named Sammy, whom I had not seen in years, but it didn't sound like him. It must be a wrong number—and yet, the person on the line addressed me by my first name.

Arabs are known for their hospitality. They will not offend or turn away visitors, even a stranger who calls or visits at an inappropriate hour. Therefore, I knew I was expected to be hospitable and welcoming to Sammy—even after midnight!

Since this man knew me by name, he could not be a total stranger. There was not one chance in a million that he had the wrong "Hanna," not in this French city. I figured he must know me, and probably expected me to know him, yet I didn't. It was an embarrassing situation, and I didn't quite know how to deal with it.

Not wanting to offend him, I responded with the same warmth of voice, greeting him back, also using his first name and acting as if he were my cousin. I asked about his dad, my uncle. He was quick to correct me. Rather than taking offense, he was elated that I had taken him for a cousin!

I came to find out that Sammy was one of our listeners. He had sent a letter or two to our office, telling us that he had a brother living in Paris, and asking for my phone number so his brother could call for spiritual counseling. I usually never gave my home number to a listener, and to this day I still wonder why I had given it to him. I had only myself to blame. My wife also had someone to blame—me! To us, home was sacred. I had learned to leave my work at the office—except this time!

Sammy was ecstatic as he shared with me brief excerpts of my message on radio that night. What I said had personally spoken to him. He felt he needed to call and thank me. The urge was so strong he didn't wait to go home. He called from his place of work—the palace of the Saudi King! The Lebanese civil war had caused him, like hundreds of thousands of other talented Lebanese workers, to leave their country and seek work abroad.

There was never a question in my mind that radio crossed national frontiers. I listened to a number of foreign stations when I lived in the Middle East myself. There also was no question that the listeners to our Christian radio programs came from all kinds of backgrounds—religious, ethnic and otherwise. I also knew that some listeners went to great lengths to secretly listen to us. But the chance of someone listening to us in a king's palace was simply extraordinary. It was like fiction coming to life!

Ahmad

I stood on the side of the road. Every time a taxi approached, I stretched out my arm. There was no sign or other indication to show if a cab was occupied or not; that could have saved me a lot of arm waving!

It was over ten minutes before a taxi stopped. That in itself was no guarantee that the driver would allow me in his car. If I was going to a part of town that conflicted with his schedule or with his commitments to other customers, he may well decide not to give me a ride. Thankfully, though, this gentleman was willing to take me.

I jumped into the car before he could change his mind. It was hot and humid outside. The car was not air-conditioned, but I was thankful at least to be on my way.

Following the general principles of our culture, and since there was a good half hour of road together, I sat in the front seat. I did not want to treat this man as a servant; besides, I wanted to chat with him. I always learn something talking to a Middle Eastern driver. They usually have the latest news. They serve a diverse clientele and pick up things that the average person may not.

Under his rearview mirror hung a small transparent plastic folder containing his driver's license. His photo and name were clearly visible: *Ahmad*. Nothing unique about that name—it is shared by millions of individuals in the world of Islam. It was one of the names of the prophet of Islam.

With a smile on my face, I greeted him, addressing him by his first name. It must have been a long day for him, and he would welcome a word of encouragement. At least that is what I thought. Regretfully, that is not how he heard it.

At my greeting, Ahmad was visibly upset. Were he not driving, he probably would have risen from his seat. For some strange reason, my words must have touched a raw nerve somewhere. Or maybe he felt threatened or offended that I used his first name. I didn't know what was going on.

He frowned, turned his attention from the road, and with a heavy local accent asked me how I knew his name. His question was threatening. It was my turn to be upset. I probably would have risen from my seat were I not in a car going fifty kilometers an hour. How could he possibly ask me that? His name was before his eyes twenty-four hours a day, seven days a week.

I did not quite know what to say. I had chosen to sit up front, as is the culture, not willing to offend him by sitting in the back. I meant to treat him as an equal—which he obviously was—rather than as someone serving me. It seemed my intentions had backfired. My greeting certainly did!

Maybe he thought I worked for the secret service. Or possibly, the revenue service! I had been caught in these uncomfortable situations before. But each time it seemed different and new! My mind raced to find a way out of this confrontation.

The seconds were running out. I had to find an answer to his threatening question. I could not frankly turn his attention to the little folder hanging down his rearview mirror. I didn't want to insult his intelligence. I put on a serious face. Serious and naive! I said, "I thought this was *your* driver's license. It seems I was wrong. Sorry for that."

The trick worked. My seeming naiveté absorbed some of his rage. I knew I was not wrong, but who cared! As long as we could talk as normal human beings, it was immaterial who was right and who was wrong. Maybe by the end of this journey we could understand each other a little better.

His reaction to my apology was as strange as his reaction to my greeting. He lifted his right hand off the steering wheel—not that he was holding it too tightly—and hit himself on the forehead. "Of course," he said. "I must be stupid." I was relieved. (I was careful not to show any outer signs of confirming or denying his statement!) I kept my peace. I wasn't sure what he had up his sleeve. I knew he was preparing to say something, but I didn't quite know what it was.

I didn't have long to wait. Not that I was ready for more of the same. But I had brought this on myself, and there was no backing off. This situation was of my own making!

There was no hesitation on his lips. He had a strategy, and he was not about to let me off the hook. He said, "What is your name?" I expected him to ask something about me, possibly where I was from, since my accent betrayed me. (I spoke Arabic, but not his dialect.)

"Hanna," I answered. "My name is Hanna." He did not seem too concerned about my family name. As it was, my first name proved to be more than enough for the next projectile. This guy was really prepared.

"How come you Christians worship three gods?" he fanatically asked. That obviously was not a question. It was not meant to be. It was an accusation. He pressed on. "This is idolatry."

I was in serious trouble—all because I dared to address him using his first name! All of a sudden, my past came back to haunt me. I remembered the friend of my youth. His name was also Ahmad.

The name may have been a coincidence, but it sure seemed like payback time! I was getting paid back for what I had done to my childhood friend, Ahmad. In my youth and in a moment of religiosity, I had accused my friend, indirectly, of lacking the truth, and had asked him if he wanted a New Testament. That question had meant the end of our relationship.

This time around, I was the one being accused—of being an idolater, of worshiping three gods! What was I to do? In my childhood, Ahmad's parents ordered him to stop seeing me. But now I was an adult, able to make my own decisions, and nobody was going to force me to stop this discussion with this driver. I was not going to give in—but I was not going to accuse either.

Thirty years had gone by since I tried to push the New Testament on Ahmad. In that time I had met and talked with many other Muslims. I have learned better. I was not going to push anything on this driver, and I was decidedly not going to argue. That, I have learned, leads absolutely nowhere.

However, I decided to answer. He had taken me off guard with his accusation; it was time I took him off guard.

"Who told you I was a Christian?" I said. "Is it because my name is Hanna? What makes you believe you are a Muslim? Just because your name is Ahmad does not necessarily make you one." I was not finished. As it was, I had barely started.

For the next five or ten minutes, I kept stressing and pressing the case that we should not be fixed on our names. Names are only means of identifying one person from another, not of identifying whether this one is a Muslim, and that one a

Christian, or anything else. In the hot religious climate of the Middle East, names are always loaded. Names, like religions, have divided people.

Ahmad listened. He agreed with some of what I said and disagreed with other things. But I was not finished. I had brought his initial reaction on myself addressing him by his first name. He was bringing this on himself by accusing me of idolatry.

One thing I have learned, and learned well, is never to argue with someone from another faith. Christ is not about religions; I am convinced He could not care less. Christ is not about safeguarding Christianity as a religious system. What Christ is all about is giving new life to people, regardless of their religion, faith or denomination.

I was not concerned about defending Christianity as an organized religion. I was concerned about the Person of Christ. Christianity cannot change people. Religion can only create religious people, and that is not Christ's purpose. He is concerned about changing human nature to be as best an imitation of Him as possible.

This is why I didn't even try to answer this man's accusation. He can think all he wants about Christians worshiping three Gods. We know we don't, but that's beside the point. I was not going to make that my central theme of defense or attack.

Ahmad and I had been in his car for about two-thirds of the way by now. Ten more minutes and I would arrive at my destination. At the start of this taxi ride, I wished I had not even taken this man's cab; now I found myself wishing we had a longer distance to travel. The discussion was taking on a new dimension. I did not want him to go before I had a

chance to tell him about what Christ meant to me and what
He could mean to him.

I know full well that presenting Christ to someone who
follows another religious system, faith or prophet can be as
challenging and as ensnaring as discussing doctrine. This is
why I hasten to say that by asking for a chance to tell Ahmad
about what Christ meant to me, I did not intend to go into
the field of Christology. This had nothing to do with Christ's
virgin birth, or with Him being One with God, or any of
the doctrinal statements or theology about Christ. This is
about the power and influence that Christ had had in my
life. This is about His power to forgive, to heal and to give
new meaning to life. If He could do that for me, He could
do it for anybody. The understanding of who Jesus really is
should come later.

Mohammed

At another time, and in another part of the Middle East,
a man in his mid-thirties or early forties was making a plea.
He was raising a prayer, every day, many times a day. He was
calling, asking, earnestly begging for help. To his chagrin,
his prayer went unanswered for years and years.

It was about midnight one night. He lay down in bed,
but not quite ready to sleep yet. He had a companion in the
room with him, one he had had for many years. Some days
he turned to this companion, some days not, depending on
his state of mind. That night he did.

He turned to his radio and turned it on. Mohammed did
not know what he was looking for. He probably wanted to
get his mind off something, rather than get it on something.
What does one do when one does not know what one wants?

This is exactly what this man did. He put the radio in his lap, and could not settle on a station. He moved across the dial right to left, and left to right. Finally, something caught his attention—a phrase, to be exact.

A number of countries of North Africa and the Middle East have seriously pushed for literacy, and have done considerably well. Others lag behind, with as much as fifty percent or more of their people unable to write, or read their own names. A weekly radio program was developed to cater to this segment of the society.

The uniqueness of this program lay in its approach. Illiterates do not necessarily compute the same way others do. Letters of the alphabet to illiterates are dead. Useless and lifeless. Their world does not have letters in them. Their world is filled with images, live images. We have turned life into a book, as I am doing now. To them life is relationships, not letters or words in a book. At the end of the day, I wonder who of us is living life to its fullness, those of us that can read and write, or those of us that cannot!

That weekly program basically used images. Each weekly episode tended to bring out one principle, one thing listeners are left with to learn. Illiterate people are not dumb. They also can compute, but in their own way. They can derive the meanings, principles and lessons that are being passed on through the diverse and colorful illustrations they hear.

Our friend Mohammed was educated, so this program for illiterates was not made for him, and significantly, the speaker did not even use the Arabic dialect most familiar to Mohammed. Nonetheless, he listened.

Every time the speaker ended one of his lively testimonies, he brought up the principle he had in mind. For fifteen minutes, our friend heard the same principle over and over again. The stories were only used to drive that one point home, and it did for this one man. "If you have a need, whatever it is, cry out to Jesus. He can meet that need. Say to Him, O Christ, the powerful."

This was not exactly what this man had been praying until now. The prayer proposed by the speaker presented innumerable intellectual challenges to him. The teaching he received all his life had said that Christ was a mere human, though a prophet. Christ, therefore, could not be present everywhere to meet our needs! To pray to Jesus was something this man could not accept, using his reason and logic. That would make Jesus nothing short of God.

But emotionally, this man was on another sphere. This was when he said to himself that he did not have anything to lose, and everything to gain, at least potentially. While his reason and logic would have completely refused to lift such a prayer, yet his emotions overpowered him. He followed his emotions rather than his reason.

Mohammed slept with those words on his lips: "O Christ, the powerful." He repeated them over and over as if they had magical power. He was probably trying to convince himself this was possible, and used his emotions to make his brain follow. Wise man! He knew that we often attach more importance to our brain than we do to our emotions, whereas we are more enslaved to our emotions than to our reason. So rather than convince himself first, which was almost impossible, and then try to subdue his emotions, he used his emotions to make his brain follow along, through repeating that phrase dozens of times.

Before dawn the next morning there was a knock on his door. Who could that be, and why would anyone come to wake him up that early? Whoever was knocking on his door sounded frantic. Mohammed opened the door and to his utter shock found his brother standing there before him.

It did not take long to understand the reason for the brother's frenzy. He could not wait to come and break the good news: Mohammed's secret wish, his one need had been met! For a minute or two, Mohammed stood at the door, staring in disbelief at his brother; his mind was elsewhere. He wondered what could have happened during the night hours to meet his need. Normally life stopped completely during the night. But not that night! Something was going on, and this man wanted an explanation.

His mind raced back to the night before. Suddenly it dawned on him. The words that he had slept with, the words that had filled his heart and mouth came back to him: "O Christ, the powerful!" His emotions had prayed, not his reason. He followed his emotions, and seemingly it worked. This Jesus was powerful. There was no other explanation. To him it all became clear. Sadly, he could not explain any of that to his brother.

By the time we heard from Mohammed, he had already started speaking to others about Christ. What was his message? The same message he had heard. The same message that had the power to meet his need! Christ was powerful!

No one had to argue his Christian faith or doctrine to convince Mohammed. Even if someone had tried, there would be fierce resistance. This man and hundreds of millions like him have been influenced by a long history that presented Christ as a good prophet sent by God. To him, and to those untold millions, Christ was *not* God; He could not be. God could not possibly become human—to become human was to become defiled.

Additionally, there was no room for the doctrine that Christians call the Trinity. God could not possibly have a son! This would be blasphemous!

All of that was now behind him, but not due to some ingenious argument! It was behind him, but not because he now understood it—as a matter of fact, he didn't. He still did not understand what the term "Son of God" meant. He did not understand how God could become human and not be defiled. But that did not matter anymore. Having seen firsthand the power of Christ to answer prayer, he chose to follow Him. The term Son of God, as it describes Christ, ceased to be the hugely debatable issue. To him, Christ was God. Nothing short of that!

That day in the Middle East, taking that momentous taxi ride, I arrived safely at my destination. Before paying what I owed Ahmad the driver, I asked him if he had a need that was not met. I asked him if he had a prayer he wished would be answered. He said yes, he did. This is when I turned to him for one last time and said, "Give Christ a try. Lift your prayer to Him. He is powerful." With that, I got out of his taxi and walked away.

I do not know what happened to the Ahmad of my high school years. Has anyone around him chosen to follow Christ, and invited him to do likewise? Oh, how I hope so! I do not know the answer to this question, but someday I will.

I also do not know what happened to the driver Ahmad. Did he lift his prayer to the powerful Christ? Oh, how I hope so! I do not know the answer to this question either, but someday I will.

I also do not know if anyone ever reached Om Ahmad, my Muslim foster mother. I say that with a lump in my throat. Oh, how I wish I had known the power of Christ in my life when I met her! But I was only full of myself, full of religion, as dead as could be! I do not know if anyone cared enough to follow Christ before her, and thereby invite her to do likewise. I am not privy to that information. How wonderful the world would be if we ceased being simply Christians—dare I say, even bigots—and learned to follow our Master: to imitate His life and love and forgiveness!

Muslims have no need for another religion. They are full to overflowing with religion. Muslims, like the rest of us, have needs the same way we do. Christ is their answer, just like Christ is our answer.

I have been asked, "Why is it that Christ appears to Muslims in visions and dreams, and not to Christians? Why is it that Christ seems to answer the prayers lifted by Muslims, and we do not hear of such among ourselves? How is it that when a Muslim sees Christ in a dream, or Christ answers his prayers, that he immediately becomes a follower of Him?"

I have said it before, but it bears repeating: Christ is *not* for Christians alone. Christ is universal. In our prejudices, we have tended to take ownership of Him, to monopolize Him. We want Him for us, and us alone. He just will not do that, to the dismay of many.

So why do we shake our heads in shock when He acts outside our Christian box? Why do we shake our heads in disbelief when He acts outside our denominational box? It is about time we learned that Christ will not be boxed in. He shocked His generation. He will continue to shock ours.

Earlier, I spoke briefly of the huge percentage of illiterates in some Middle Eastern and North African countries. I gave an example of a radio program that caters to this segment of the Arab society. That program had to be made. It had to be different, because the illiterate society thinks differently. They compute differently. They do not necessarily follow the Greek methodology that we have been taught to use in our educational systems.

We can think of Christ's appearances to the Muslims in the same way. To us who are literate, Christ will speak to us through a book—through *the* Book, the Bible—and not necessarily through a dream! If Christ were to appear to me in a dream, I would not even recognize Him. Why would He therefore speak to me in that way?

There is another element. Muslims are predisposed to dreams. They are predisposed to the influence of dreams and visions, whereas many of us are not. That should be ample explanation. Because our Muslim friends are predisposed to dreams, they will act on what they see and interpret, much more than we would through the influence of a good book, or any other means. Their dreams take on the size of life itself. It is visual, and not virtual. It becomes part of their spiritual reality. Many simply act on it, waking up to say, to our amazement and their own, that they have become followers of Christ. They may not be "Christian," but they are followers of Christ. Here they have a lot to teach us, and we have a lot to learn.

19

9/11

I WAS in my late teens before I discovered my true birth date. The convent in Bethany where I had been sent as a child had more serious issues to deal with than celebrating the birthdays of the boys they were caring for. Birthdays were a non-issue.

At age twelve I ran away from the convent. I had had it. I forced myself on my family despite their very meager means. It was during the few years that followed that the issue surfaced for the first time. As it was, no one in my family could remember when it was that I was born. June 24 was the patron day of St. John. Since Hanna is Arabic for John, I convinced myself that June 24 must be my birthday. Still, I did not celebrate it. But at least I had a date I could give for my birthday if asked.

I finished my high school education and was waiting for my student visa to arrive. I had been promised a scholarship at a Catholic university in the USA. The visa never came. In the process, I had asked for and was issued a Jordanian passport. This is when I discovered my true birth date, and it was not June 24, as I had assumed and claimed all those years.

The officer checking the birth records knew my birth date was not June 24. I argued with him, and tried to get him to change the records. For obvious reasons, I could not convince him. Later, a fateful day in Vienna made me wish I had succeeded.

The date was September 11, 2001. I was in Vienna for the umpteenth time. It had become customary for me to be in Vienna at about the same time every year. We had business meetings the day before and more planned for that day and the day to follow. There was nothing special about it, except for one thing: It was my birthday. For some strange reason, it had completely slipped my mind until a colleague said to me in passing, "Happy Birthday!"

At about three that afternoon the whole team sang "Happy Birthday" to me. Fifteen minutes later, the meetings resumed. Shortly after, the double doors leading to our meeting room were flung open, and a colleague's wife came crashing through. She was out of breath. She came down two flights of stairs running. Something was seemingly very wrong.

Without stopping to breathe, she turned to me and said, "Hanna, your wife called from the USA!" My head turned. Why would my wife call? And why couldn't this sister wait for dinner time to tell me about this call? And why did she bother, at her age, to come running down two flights of stairs? Evelyn couldn't possibly have called to wish me a happy birthday. She knew I would be in meetings. I had attended such meetings in previous years during my birthday and she never called. Why today?

There must be another reason. Evelyn had recently received her driver's license. She was a new driver. Was she involved in a car accident? I stood to my feet. But before I could ask my question, this sister said, "The USA is under attack!"

Suddenly nothing on our agenda seemed important anymore. Everyone ran up to the second floor. Others of our staff had preceded us. In this office was the only television in the building. All eyes were fixed on it. The tapes were being replayed over and over. The pictures hit us like lightning. Two planes had crashed into the World Trade Center in New York. A third had hit the Pentagon, and a fourth was downed in a field in Pennsylvania. No one knew if any more were coming!

It seemed the end was near. What we were watching was out of this world. No one had dared to do anything close to what our eyes were seeing—not anywhere or anytime. The USA proved much more vulnerable than most were willing to admit. Every sense of security dissipated. Nothing under the sun was safe anymore.

Everyone waited for the verdict. Everyone wanted to know who the guilty party was. It would not be long before the fingers were pointed at Arab Islamic fundamentalists.

We stood for about two hours with our eyes glued to the screen. We then returned to the meeting room, not to meet, but to pray. There was nothing else we could do. We were at the end of ourselves. There was no way to turn but upward.

Everyone in the group prayed. I did not. I could not. My world had just been shattered. What I had set out to do over thirty years ago was being destroyed in a matter of minutes! And when? On my very birthday, September 11! Something inside me died that day.

I had set out to repay two debts. My first debt was to Om Ahmad, the Muslim woman who nursed me when my mother was dying of cancer. My other debt was to God, for keeping our family safe during the Six-Day War of 1967. God kept His end of the bargain that day. I had kept my end of it all those years since.

I had dedicated my life to minister to the Arab and Muslim peoples of North Africa and the Middle East. In July of 1971, my ministry was launched out of a basement in Beirut, Lebanon. Thirty years and two months later, on my birthday, I discovered that I had failed miserably. That part of the world did not become a better place as a result of my ministry. On the contrary! Now it exported death and destruction. The big question that faced me was whether I had been wasting my time all these years.

As the events of September 11 unfolded, I lumped all the Muslims in the same boat. For a while, every Muslim became another Osama Bin Laden. For a while I seemed to have lost my vision and, more importantly, my love! Those strong sentiments of indebtedness to Om Ahmad seemed to go up in smoke. I was convinced it was all very futile.

My birth date was ruined forever. Not that I had celebrated every time the date came around—even on that marked day in 2001, I had forgotten it was my birthday. That evening I called home from Vienna and spoke briefly to my wife to check on her and encourage her. I also said to myself and to her that it would be the last birthday celebration I ever have. I promised that on my next, I would be all dressed in black! I clothed myself in apathy and indifference, both inside and out!

I was tormented in my soul. Where once I had thought

that love for my neighbor reigned supreme, I was harboring feelings of distrust, almost hate. My mind and my will did not want to give in to those feelings. I did not want to allow myself to turn into an agent of hate like those men that brought death and destruction on that morning of September 11. Giving in to hate could not possibly be God's will for me; but my emotions kept getting in the way.

Months went by. My sense of failure gave way to discouragement, and discouragement to indifference. I began considering what else in life I wished I had done, and what things in life I wished I could do. I had had odd jobs in my youth. I worked as a tourist guide in the Old city of Jerusalem. I was always good with directions. My wife is convinced that if she broke open my skull, she would find maps inside. I could succeed as a taxi driver. I could also succeed as a salesman. I did that working for the travel agency in Amman, Jordan. That would probably be easier on my back than driving a taxi.

My wife of thirty years would not hear any of this. While still away in Europe waiting for the airports in the USA to reopen after those attacks, Evelyn had stayed in bed three days crying. As an Arab she identified herself with those madmen, and took their guilt on herself. But she knew that giving in was not the answer. She had answered God's call on her life to serve Him in her late teens while on her deathbed. She was not going to give up on her call, and neither was she going to let me give up on mine. She said to wait on God and pray. He would guide us through.

Long before the infamous September 11, Evelyn said to me again and again that our ministry lacked hands and feet. It was mostly tongue—talk. It was good talk, but talk nonetheless. In her answer to God's call, she had wanted to be a missionary to serve children in need. It didn't matter where. It was the *what*: the type of ministry. I had turned a deaf ear to what she yearned to do. It seemed life was going around what I wanted, and definitely not what she wanted. Could it be that God was using 9/11 to change our course of ministry altogether?

I spent considerable hours alone—alone with God and my memories. I remembered Mustapha, the young soldier, standing along the road asking for a ride. I remembered how he had stretched his hand to shake mine. Most of all I remembered his words: "Brother Hanna," he said, "I will see you in heaven." I was a brother to Mustapha. *He* had called me brother.

I also remembered Omar. Omar and his friend. Their dark-skinned faces and their shabby looks were before me. They had lost three of their friends, their family and their country. They were asylum seekers. They endured all that simply because they wanted to follow Christ.

Many other faces were before me in my study day after day. Faces with names and faces without names! Some were from a Christian background and others from a Muslim background.

Suddenly I realized there was absolutely no difference between them. They were all my brothers and sisters in Christ. There were no barriers. Christ had removed the barriers, and we keep constantly trying to put them back.

I felt ashamed of myself. I was turning my back on my brothers and sisters. I was betraying them. I had led some into a relationship with the living Christ, and now with my prejudices, I was denying His power. I was sinning against

God and against my brothers! There were still corners of ugly sinfulness lurking in my heart, and I was in need of forgiveness, just like the first day I asked for it in that basement in East Jerusalem.

Alone with God many months after 9/11, my heart went out to my Muslim brothers and sisters, those who had chosen, at great cost, to become followers of Christ. I prayed. I asked for Christ's forgiveness. Tears of repentance ran down my cheeks. I promised I would never forget them again.

Between me and my God, I made a new vow. For over thirty years I had dedicated my life to lead others to follow Christ; now I promised I would walk alongside those who made that decision. Except this shall no longer be my ministry. It shall be our ministry—as much Evelyn's as mine. Together we will be hands and feet to children, to women, to anyone God puts in our way. We want to help as many as possible among the followers of Christ to continue seeking Him—to endure whatever the cost!

To be continued . . .